I0059803

The Beginners'
Guide to
Wealth Creation

The Beginners' Guide to Wealth Creation

Taiwo **ADESINA** & Kehinde **ADESINA**

Copyright Notice

Copyright © 2008 Taiwo Adesina, Kehinde Adesina

1ˢᵗ Edition—2008

Republished—2013

ISBN: 978-1-909787-00-1

Published by Purpose2Destiny TK Limited

All rights reserved. Any unauthorized broadcasting, public performance, copying or recording will constitute an infringement of copyright. Permission granted to reproduce for personal and educational use only. Commercial copying, hiring, lending is prohibited.

Some Authors have been quoted or referred to in this book, their rights are preserved and the writers of this book do not seek to infringe on those rights.

This work is registered with the UK Copyright Service

Exclusion of Liability and Disclaimer

The information in this book has been obtained from various sources. The information in this book is not and should not be construed as financial advice and may not necessarily take your individual situation into account. You are advised to consult with an Independent Financial Adviser, Consultant or Relevant Agency before implementing any action.

We cannot guarantee your future results. There are unknown risks when carrying out any financial strategies or transactions, some of which are mentioned in this book which the authors have no control over. This book is meant to guide you through the wealth building process.

The authors shall have neither liability nor responsibility to any person or entity with respect to any loss or damage caused or alleged to be caused directly or indirectly by the information covered in this Book.

Although careful precaution has been taken in the preparation of this material, the authors assume no liability for any incidental, consequential or other liability from the use of this information. All risks and damages, incidental or otherwise, arising from the use or misuse of the information contained herein are entirely the responsibility of the reader.

Dedication

This book is dedicated to our family members near and far—to the Adesinas, Oshins, Shobandes and Adeyemos.God has given you all the treasures of the land; the riches stored in secret places and the wealth of nations; take possession of His blessings.

To the readers of this book—may the insight you gain transform your lives for ever.

Acknowledgment

We thank Dr Malcolm Havard, an economist and real estate professional with 25 years experience, for editing this second edition. We thank Ingela Troha for her initial editing of this Manuscript. Ingela has over 18 years experience in the Financial Services Industry.

Photography by Gemsjummy, Jumoke Ademola has been a professional photographer for many years.

Contents

Preface

It is one thing for a person to decide they want to embark on the road to financial freedom but yet another to follow through with that decision as it often takes guts, determination and persistence. In a nutshell, it is about changing both one's internal and external worlds. Be prepared to work your hands as it will be worth your while!

If you are sick and tired of being where you are at the moment and want to achieve Financial Success, then you must really desire CHANGE in your life. We do not want you to be disillusioned; we want you to know that you MUST start doing things differently to achieve the new results you desire.

Albert Einstein said;

> *"The definition of insanity is doing the same thing but expecting different results".*

All great achievers start with an idea, but it is the burning desire within them that turns their idea into reality. The idea is only a short-term inspiration. It is the burning desire within you that gives you the tenacity to overcome any unavoidable obstacles along your way. Obstacles are simply challenges which you don't yet have the skill-set to either overcome or manage.

We will be honest by cautioning you now. The major reason people fail in their quest for financial freedom is that they retreat or crumble as soon as they come against any type of adversity.

Their expectations were clouded by illusions, as they did not expect to come up against any obstacles. Expect obstacles and treat them as challenges, then you won't be taken by surprise and feel discouraged. Challenges will develop your skill set and expand your level of awareness. Do not be afraid of the unknown, or ponder too long on the "how" as this can become a stumbling block.

Procrastination is the killer of many dreams. Start working towards your new goal with the knowledge that you currently have, and as you go along you will see new ways and gain new insight for the next step. Too often we think that we need to have all information to hand before starting out, but this is not true as this prevents people from starting.

Retrain yourself to anticipate that most aspects of your new goals will be unknown until after you have taken the first step. Being faced with many "unknowns" should be exciting. Be confident that even if you don't know the answer now you will know it as you go along.

Most importantly, if you are **specific** on WHERE you want to go and WHAT you want to achieve, it will be easier for you to 'see' the answers and information you are looking for. A great analogy is of the driver who drove at night from one city to another with his headlights on. When he started his journey he was only able to see 20 metres in front of him, however as he drove along he kept seeing further 20 metres until he arrived at his destination. This is exactly how it works with your goals . . . you uncover the "how" with each new step you take.

You will never know all the intricate details at the outset of your journey and even if you know them they often change as you progress.

If you want to become a millionaire then you need to start THINKING & ACTING like one. This does not mean that you have to become an academic; it simply means that you need to develop your mindset so that you can begin to have the expectations and discipline of a millionaire.

In order to create an abundance of wealth you need to undertake a journey of self-discovery and self-appraisal. This journey will take you on the road less travelled. If you follow the crowd you will only achieve their level of success and nothing more.

Statistics show that around 97% of people live at or below average whilst a tiny 3% rise above the average to experience all the wonders that this world can offer. Make sure you are part of this minority!

Expect great things and you will **receive** great things as <u>you are worthy of it.</u>

Chapter 1

The Wealth Journey

The Wealthy Road

If you want to become wealthy in every area of your life then the best place to start is by learning from someone who has travelled the same road that you want to take.

If you were to ask people who inherited their wealth why they are wealthy, they wouldn't be able to provide you with an in-depth response for you to gain any beneficial insight to turn your life around. They may tell you how they got their wealth but they can't advice you on how to <u>create</u> and <u>retain</u> wealth. However, if you were to ask people who steadily built up their wealth, they would have a lot to tell you on how to create and retain wealth.

The Wealthy Mind

Thousands of people desire a life different to what they currently have. They dream of more love, more time and more valuable items as they believe these would make their lives more comfortable. In the world we live in today **. . . we all have an insatiable desire for more . . . .**

Wealth creation starts at a subconscious level; this is why it can be so hard to turn around one's conscious mind. If you truly want to increase your wealth then get ready for the most interesting journey of your life. Understand that once you change your subconscious mind that your external world will change too. Have the courage to do whatever it takes to break through those internal barriers that have been limiting you.

You must have a passion to succeed and to influence those around you positively, however passion alone is insufficient rather determination and drive will cause you to attain the financial freedom you desire. You must dream big to get big results. Stretch your imagination and let your mind expand to reach the limit it is capable of reaching.

The difference between a person who creates wealth and one who just dreams of creating wealth is in the extra effort the former puts in. Motivated wealth creators are tenacious, focused and committed to achieving their financial goals. They understand that procrastinating is costly so they are diligent in understanding the seasons of life and act promptly.

You must have a clear objective of where you want to go. What you do daily will have an impact on what you achieve. Your daily habits are indicative of your future. To succeed in life you must truly believe that you will succeed. If you have a defeatist mentality from the beginning then there is no need in starting out at all as you will gravitate towards your thoughts.

You must understand at the outset that it will take you time to build your wealth so don't be too hard on yourself. Have a balanced view of yourself and your capabilities. There are skills you don't have yet which are required to achieve your vision, when you take one step at a time you will build these skills. The accumulation of wealth is progressive; forget the get rich quick schemes as those who take shortcuts suffer the consequences.

You alone are in control of your destiny, you are in the driver's seat, and wherever you direct the steering wheel you will find yourself. You must understand who you are, what you stand for and where you expect to end up. Don't allow others to determine the course of your life. Have confidence in yourself. Keep your dreams aflame. It is never too late to create the financial future you desire.

It is simply not enough to have a wealthy mind;
inaction will make your mind redundant.

Limiting Beliefs

We limit ourselves by holding on to negative beliefs that do not take us anywhere. We also allow others to limit us by giving them the power to decide whether or not we are capable of achieving our dreams. To step on to the platform of life, we need to let go of everything and everyone that limits our capabilities.

These beliefs could be in the form of internal conversations that we sometimes have with ourselves, such as;

"I'm too old; I'm too tired; I'm too young; I'm not good looking enough; I'm not smart enough; that's too hard; they wouldn't let me"

Or . . .

"I can't do that because of my race; my gender; my disability" . . . .

These thoughts play like a CD player which is stuck on the continuous 'loop' mode inside of our heads. These are some of the reasons we give for not doing the things we would love to do.

"It is a very funny thing about life –If you refuse to accept anything
but the best you very often get it."
—W. Somerset Maugham
(1874-1965, Novelist and Playwright)

Walt Disney took action by investing in the financial future he desired for himself and his descendants. He saw financial freedom and went for it. He created Disney World, a legacy which is still with us today. You must believe that despite your current financial situation you can change your financial standing. Always have a wealthy mindset despite the setbacks and hiccups you encounter on the way to your financial freedom.

Being single or being a single parent is not a bar to you grasping and reaching for what you desire. J K Rowling, the author of the Harry Porter series was a single parent when she started writing earnestly. Despite this, she did not allow anything to hamper her progress in life.

Your desire to succeed must be stronger than your current limitations. Having the right mindset is a pre-requisite to keeping your momentum. Are you really serious about fulfilling your financial goals? If you are, then start right now so that you can maximise the time you have in your hands and become all that you were destined to be.

As parents you must train your children to have a wealthy mindset; to respect money and to have a drive to be financially independent when they become adults.

If you are a young person then you have time on your hands to start creating the financial dream you want for tomorrow. It is much easier to recondition your mind now than later. Having a wealthy and positive mindset goes a long way to setting yourself up on your path to financial freedom. Get yourself involved in the family finances, ask your parents to allow you to make some financial decisions at home, this way you will be in a position to manage your finances when you leave home.

There are many children and young adults who became millionaires before the age of 25. Some of these young millionaires are:

- **Ben Casnocha** of Comcate.Ben. At 17 years old he was named one of the nations top 25 entrepreneurs under 25 by Business Week;
- **Stephen Yellin** at 13 years of age was writing and talking politics
- **Ashley Qualls** of Whateverlife.com became a millionaire by the age of 25.

Their full biography can be found at http://abcnews.go.com/Technology/PCWorld/story?id=4417827.

- And, in March 2013, **Nick D'Aloisio,** aged 17 years sold his Summlyap application to Yahoo for millions of pounds, see http://www.guardian.co.uk/technology/2013/mar/29/summly-creator-nick-daloisio-interview.

You can therefore see that age is no barrier to building and creating wealth. Limiting beliefs are the excuses we give to ourselves or to others for not making progress or achieving anything in life.

A great story that shows how our 'beliefs' control our actions on a day to day basis was where a TV programmer decided to put a man on a busy street of a major city with a couple of brief cases full of cash and a sign that read "FREE MONEY". The man was instructed that if anyone asked him for money he was to give them what they asked for.

It came as a surprise to the TV programmer that over the course of the day only one person asked the man for money for a train ticket. Everyone else read the sign and simply walked around him. Some gave him a weird look and others didn't even seem to notice that he was there. We can see that people were reacting to the situation based on their beliefs that . . .

"Money is never free."
"There must be a catch."
"Who is that loony? He must be crazy."
"This is too good to be true."

The interesting thing was that the man had enough money in his brief cases to cancel a lot of people's debts, if only they had asked him for some. You can see how your beliefs can limit you to the various opportunities available to you every single day.

Self Image (Self Schema)

If you are one of those who have attended numerous Personal Development seminars, have a library of self-development books & DVDs as long as your arms and are still not achieving your desired results, then you have not fully understood that it is your Self Image that controls your destiny.

So what is "Self Image" and how do we know what our own Self Image is?

Self Image is the mental picture each individual has of themself at the <u>subconscious level</u>. It is easy to 'see' when you know what to <u>look</u> for in your self.

Our SELF IMAGE = the current results we are achieving in every facet of our lives.

If someone drives around in a second hand car that is always breaking down; can barely afford their rent or put quality wholesome food on their table; has a low income and continuously moves from one relationship to another, then these level of achievement in each area makes up their Self Image, (these are the expectations the individual has of what they can achieve).

An example which clearly portrays the Self Image of people from different groups is as follows:-

A man puts an advertisement in a national newspaper looking for a Sales Representative. The advertisement stated that the successful applicant must have a passion for sales and be highly driven etc, whilst no particular qualifications were essential. The salary on offer was around £95,000. Only three people nationwide responded to the advertisement. As a result of the low response the man decided to run the same advert a few weeks later and changed **only** the salary to read £15,000.

To the man's amazement so many candidates applied that he was inundated with the high number of responses and was unable to cope. You can see how peoples' self belief affected their self worth as they only responded to an advert offering £15,000 rather than £95,000.

We all want more money, but why is it that some people are being paid much more for a similar or exactly the same position? The answer is simple, people **accept <u>less</u> than what they are worth because they don't feel good about themselves or they think they don't deserve the best.**

Of course we must give value in our service that is equal to the salary/payment we receive. All dealings must be of fair exchange, each party must feel they have received or given something equal to the money paid.

So, what if you were to ask a person to describe their Self Image, would they clearly articulate it?

If you do not understand the importance of having a good Self Image, you could easily short change yourself. Many people would describe their Self Image as what they consciously think about themselves.

A person who is generally happy with both their mental abilities and physical appearance, and has a "can do" attitude, would give and reflect a positive description of their 'self-image' whilst a person who feels that they are unintelligent, ugly and a failure would give a negative description of their self-image.

What if a person only has a £15,000 per annum job, £0 savings, significant credit card debts, second hand car, and buys their clothes in a second hand store? Should that justify a person saying that he/she is a failure? Definitely not!

The wealthy person would never describe himself negatively despite facing set backs because he knows that his situation is only temporal and that he would soon come out of the adverse situation. The results you are achieving in every facet of your life are a reflection of your **SELF IMAGE and BELIEF you hold about yourself.**

To identify what your EXACT Self Image is, **all** <u>you need to do is to look at the current results in your life right now.</u> what type of car do you drive; how many investments do you have; how is your relationship with your partner, friends & family?; what is your home like; what is the balance of your savings (if any); what is your lifestyle like, are you at your desired destination? If not, what actions are you taking to get there?

So regardless of what we say to ourselves or other people, our true self image is clearly reflected in the results we are achieving. Your current results reflect all the decisions that you have been making and what you believe you can achieve.

It is very important to understand that you can NEVER outperform your Self Image, and until you change your Self Image you will not achieve your desired results.

This is why people who leave an abusive relationship quickly find themselves in another abusive relationship. Their Self Image tells them that they deserve the abuse, as this negative feeling is engraved in their subconscious mind.

This brings us to the next question; how do we condition our mindset positively in order to have a good Self Image?

Mindset conditioning (habits)

Conditioning is an amazing characteristic trait in Humans that allows them to effectively function at a higher level in their daily lives than any other specie. As adults we take conditioning for granted. If you watch young children you will see how important conditioning is in your life and more importantly the right form of conditioning. The basic forms of conditioning can be explained through examples such as;

- *Putting* your trousers/blouse on . . . We do this daily without even thinking about it, but watch an infant who has not yet been taught (conditioned) which area of the body to wear his/her trousers on, he/she will more likely try to put his/her trousers/blouse on his/her head or arms.
- *What* about when you brush your teeth . . . You barely need to think about what you are doing, but a small child is likely to chew the tooth brush. An adult would also find brushing their teeth just as complex as a child would if they weren't ever taught to brush their teeth.
- *Even* walking . . . As simple as this one sounds, it is something most of us take for granted unless it is taken away. Those injured in car crashes need to go through a rehabilitation process to be taught to walk again. It often takes months of frustration before they re-learn how to walk again. They state that re-learning to walk is one of the hardest things they have had to learn.

Our walking movements are so ingrained into our subconscious mind, that when we want to move to the other side of the room, we just get up and walk. We aren't consciously thinking . . . ok now stand up, now move all the hundreds of different muscles & coordinate the left & right sides of our body to walk across the room. Our subconscious mind is controlling everything to create the smooth function of walking.

So what does CONDITIONING have to do with earning lots of money? Well it has a lot because how we treat money steams from how we were conditioned as children. That is why most people who were brought up in a positive/wealthy household have no problem in creating and multiplying their wealth. It is part of their way of life.

Conditioning impacts everything we do in life, from the way we talk (different accents and languages is simply a form of conditioning), the way we eat, what we eat, the way we socialise, and of course the way we handle money. As there are wealthy people from all walks of life, gender, race and religion we can't give the excuse that we are from a minority group so therefore we are unable to obtain & retain wealth. Some defend their position by saying "Oh, but they are just lucky!" No, that is definitely not the case.

As we will highlight later, majority of the "lotto" winners spend all or most of their winnings within three years and are back to where they started.

This goes to show that majority of the "lucky people" are not able to RETAIN THEIR WEALTH, this is because they have not conditioned their mindsets and are still thinking like the poor who often only think of the present rather than their future.

To <u>obtain & retain</u> wealth you need to integrate successful strategies into your every day life by REPETITION, until they become a HABIT. Once these new strategies become ingrained you will have a new Self Image as you would have successfully reconditioned your mindset to think like the wealthy (wealth building strategies are discussed in chapter 4 of this book).

When actions become a habit things become easier as they are part of you and what you do. This is why it is very difficult for some people to change their MONEY HABITS as conditioning of their habits require having a complete change of their mindset at the subconscious level. If you don't overwrite your old habits with new habits you will keep achieving the same results resulting in stagnancy.

Breaking habits is probably the hardest thing you will ever do in your life. The majority of cigarette smokers find it hard to quit, the good news is that it is not impossible and it does get easier and easier as time goes on.

Focus on the results that you want to achieve and keep moving forward. This is why we began this book by stating that you will need to carry out a self-appraisal of your current money habits and replace them with new habits. Design the new results you desire to see in your life.

ACTION STRATEGY:-

To effectively get rid of a habit, it is virtually impossible to simply stop the action. You need to actually replace it with a new action. For example; a smoker could exchange smoking for exercising. You need to replace a destructive habit with a new positive one that would take you closer to your goal. Therefore, a lot of reflection is needed in order to make that change.

Levels of Awareness

A turning point in your life will be when you fully understand the different 'levels of awareness' in your mind.

Levels of awareness are simply the extent at which you understand things, their functions and interaction with other things in your world.

The lowest level of awareness is found in animals:—If a dog is in a car it knows that it is in a car, but it doesn't know that it knows that it is in a car; whereas human beings know that they know that they are in a car. (We have an awareness of 'self')

The dog also has no concept of how the car functions; it just knows that it is in something that moves occasionally. Majority of people know that a car is a motor vehicle powered by an engine that runs on gas/petrol. However, majority of people wouldn't understand the intricate functions of an engine, how it is assembled or the complexity of the engineering involved. Their level of awareness about motor vehicles does not extend to that higher level.

Each of us has varying degrees of awareness of the concepts that make up our world. Having a higher level of awareness allows you to 'see' more of the bigger picture and the interconnections between things.

A lower level of awareness affects the development of the Self Image because one would accept failure and simultaneously blame other people, events & circumstances (external influences) for the situation they find themselves in.

"There are no limitations to the mind except those we acknowledge; both poverty and riches are the offspring of thought."
—Napoleon Hill, From Think and Grow Rich

You must be aware of the creative powers residing within you and tap them so that you can become resourceful. You must change your perception of life by thinking outside the box.

Even with an extremely positive outlook on life people still settle for second best because they haven't conditioned their mindsets at the subconscious level to go only for the best. Why do people often buy second hand cars when they can easily walk into a dealer's shop and ask for a new car (knowing that they can afford to do so); why do people go to a dealer that sells the averaged priced new car; Why not shop at a luxury vehicle dealer such as BMW, Chrysler, Mercedes-Benz, Porsche?

People are not fully aware of how their conditioning affects their outlook on life.

People say, "I just want a car to get me from point A to point B". But why not go from A to B in pure comfort? Don't shiver and shake in a car with no heating, or sweat profusely in a car with no air conditioning. Instead imagine yourself driving your dream car and having your ultimate driving experience.

Go to your nearest luxury car dealer and take a car for a test drive to experience the difference between driving a normal car from a luxurious car. It is certain that once someone experiences something better they will never want to go back to where they are coming from.

Ask yourself this, what is your current annual income? How long have you been in this sort of income bracket? When you last looked for a new job what was your selection criteria? Did you apply for any jobs that were advertised at £95,000 per annum? If not, why not? The reason is you simply were not aware of how you could earn £95,000 per annum!

What is the difference between someone who earns £95,000 per annum and a person who earns £9,500 per annum? It is their level of awareness & self image that controls their earning capability. The £9,500 per annum earner definitely holds the belief that the only way he can earn <u>more money</u> is to work <u>more hours</u>. By holding on to this belief he is limiting his capability.

Your Attitude & Choices

"Our attitudes control our lives. Attitudes are a secret power working 24 hours a day for good or bad. It is of paramount importance that we know how to harness and control this great force."
—*Tom Blandi, Author.*

Earlier on we mentioned that when a person has a lower level of awareness he blames other people, events & circumstances (external influences) for the situations he find himself in and the results he is achieving. The individual does not realise that the outcomes in his life are **not all** due to external forces, but by the **choices and decisions** he has made.

You don't need anyone's permission to succeed in life but yourself. Wealth does not happen by chance but by time, effort and action. Don't give up when you face temporary setbacks. You cannot be lazy and expect to see real changes. It is not about overworking yourself to the ground but rather it is by applying sound financial principles.

Every person's perception of a situation is different, as our perceptions are based upon our belief system (conditioning); that is why individuals make different decisions even though they face the same circumstances.

The main distinction between achievers and non achievers is that achievers are **brave enough to learn new ideas and concepts**. They make the decision to learn and develop their skills set, especially their financial knowledge. Non achievers fail to expand their knowledge and have an attitude that things are too hard. We have the power to choose our attitude in every situation that we might find ourselves in.

. . . having a good attitude will:-

- Enable you succeed in every sphere of your life;
- Make you healthier;
- Allow you to make informed decisions;
- Strengthen your relationships;
- Reduce your stress levels.

. . . . making the right choices will result in you:-

- Saving money;
- Saving time and effort;
- Getting the best deals that is of fair and equal exchange;
- Reducing wastage;
- Maximising output;
- Being effective.

Wealth Psychology

In order to start thinking the right way about money you need to have the right wealth psychology. There are certain rules about money which are worth learning. These are:

Value

Money has a time value. Cash now is always worth more than cash in the future. You must be sure that the return is worth it if you are getting paid at some point in the future. What would you prefer, £100 now or £100 in the future? That is easy; you should choose the £100 now. But what if you were offered the choice of £100 now or £110 later? That is more difficult, you will need to know what return you can get on the money. If you can only get a 5%

return over the year then the most you could get by the end of the year is £105, so you should take the £110. If you can invest the money and get 15%, 20% or more, then you need the money now. You will make a profit on the deal.

Be aware of the effect of inflation and real interest rates. If you see an attractive interest rate on a savings – say 5%—that may seem to be a good place to put your money. If, however, inflation (the measure of how prices are changing in the economy) is at 7%, putting your money in this account will see its net worth go DOWN by 2% every year. This may seem unlikely but note that it has been difficult recently to get rates on simple savings accounts of more than 1-2% and inflation has been at around 3%. Real interest rates are negative.

Equity is better than debt. This does not mean that you should ignore debt (debt can be good in a rising market) but in fact equity, the bit you actually own, can be used to lever more funds. The best way of illustrating this is if you have £100,000 in cash you can buy a single property (flat) outright if your property is situated outside London. If you let/rent that out you may get approx £500 a month in rent. That's a 6% annual return. Let's look at an alternative; you can split the cash into four parts of £25,000 each and put a deposit down on four flats/apartments. Each of these can also be let/rented out at approx £6000 per annum giving you a total income of £24,000. Even after interest charges on the mortgages and payments of service charges the net income produced will be much higher than purchasing a single property. You will now have four assets for capital gains when property values rise again.

Control

Money is best when you can have free control over it. The best illustration of this is the difference in interest rates between easy access accounts (ones you can withdraw money from at any time) and term accounts (where you are required to keep the money untouched for a set period). The longer the term the higher the rate of interest you will get.

These rules apply to any situation where money can be earned. The best returns are usually to be found on long-term projects but these mean losing control of your money for longer periods of time as it is tied up. The downside is that if other opportunities come along you cannot react to them easily. People who have put all of their money into their houses are often wealthy on paper but do not have much cash flow.

Where you put your money tends to be a compromise between return and access. This is an area where you need to make a very careful analysis of what your needs are.

Invest

Money can be scarce sometimes. We all know how difficult it can be to make money during a recession, however we need to make the most efficient use of what we have; money should be worked. This means putting it where it will give a good return i.e. it should be invested. Money tucked under the mattress is effectively reducing in value by the hour because of the effect of inflation. The same is true of money kept in a current account. If you regularly have a surplus in your current account you are actually watching your personal wealth reduce in value as you do not get any return.

That said it is worse when you always have to borrow money. As we have already seen, borrowing money can be good if you are using the funds to invest in assets that have the potential to appreciate in value i.e. property or gold or to fund the development of something that can earn you a long term income like a new business, but if you are using it just to fund your downward investments like cars, I-pads, flat-screen TV's, all of which steadily reduce in value, then all you are doing is setting yourself on a spiral of wealth reduction.

Make

Making money during a recession can be tough but there are always opportunities out there which can give you the opportunity to make more. This can be in a variety of ways such as making a full-time career change, moving from being employed to running your own business, finding part-time money making ventures by utilising your skills or hobbies, setting up an e-bay business and/or finishing with more passive money making tools via investments.

Which method is right for you depends upon you as a person and your particular circumstances, however some lateral thinking can open up some very rewarding avenues.

Protect

For the un-savvy, Money can be sometimes hard to keep. People who have the best track record of making and keeping money have a good understanding of one key factor: Risk.

Risk and return are inextricably linked. Risky ventures are the ones that give the greatest return. If we look at things like comparing the returns on Building Society savings accounts and playing the Stock Market, the potential returns of the latter are clearly much higher but investors run the risk of losing everything should the companies they invest in go bust whilst the money in the savings account is safe (indeed, after the financial crisis and Northern Rock losses) as they are protected by a government guarantee. Similarly, venture capitalists like Dragon's Den know that two out of three investments they make will fail, however the one that will succeed will give them 30% or more returns. Companies go to the venture capitalists knowing that it will cost them a much higher percentage of their future profits as most High Street banks are not willing to run the risk of losing their money should the business fail.

One important rule to remember is nothing is risk free. If some idea or venture is sold to you as being this, or the return looks to be very high compared with the level of risk that they say it has, then it is almost certainly too good to be true.

Know your risks. Weigh up whether the return you might get is worth the risk that you are running. That is one of the key ways to protecting your money.

Asset protection

As well as risk, there are other actions that you can take to protect your money. One is to mitigate risk i.e. spread the risk around; the other is to insure the risk, where possible, against loss of your earnings or profit.

We all know the principles of risk spreading; the old adage 'never put all your eggs into one basket' rings true. Investing in one thing or pursuing just one business idea can leave you exposed if that one market or project goes wrong. The more 'spread' you have, the less risk to your wealth.

You cannot always insure against loss, particularly in investment (although really sophisticated investors and big companies do so by using futures markets and hedge funds), but you can protect yourself against loss of crucial assets such as your earnings – your car, your computer, any premises you have, your stock etc, and you can also insure against claims being taken out against you by taking out public liability and professional indemnity insurance. Insurance is always a trade-off between cost and benefit; insurance can be expensive, however, it is essential that you protect your assets/wealth.

Save

Saving is a good habit, as long as you follow the rules about money's time value and the investment rule. Savings provide investment funds; one of the reasons that Japan was so successful in the post-war period was that its population were seasoned savers; this gave Japanese banks the funds to plough into their industries.

Saving should be active; you should always review whether you are getting an adequate return on your investment. It should also be for a purpose; you should try and save FOR something. And remember that the best way of saving is investment.

Money does not need to dominate your life, however you must understand that Money is powerful; those with money rule the world. Money opens up opportunities as it not only gives you a better quality of life but also allows you to do good for others. Bill and Melissa Gates are examples of Billionaires who have used their wealth for good and charitable purposes. They give their wealth out through their charitable foundations; they have become a force for good in the world.

Just like the Gates, you too can become a force for good and change the world; you can only do this when you have the right psychology about wealth and money. You can improve not only your own life but the lives of those around you.

Investor Psychology

We started this book by discussing the mindset as it a **crucial component to creating wealth**. The KEY to creating wealth is not the particular investment vehicle or the particular strategy used, so searching for that perfect golden strategy or investment scheme is not going to get you rich (not for long anyway), rather it is having and maintaining the right mindset.

- Investor psychology means the "MENTAL HABITS OF THE INVESTOR".
- The investor's psychology accounts for 80-90% of their success.
- Therefore, if you have not identified and got rid of your 'old' mental habits and imbibe 'new' mental habits in their place, you won't have much success in maintaining a <u>LASTING CHANGE</u>.

All Master Investors spend **more** time studying and improving on their psychology than they do learning new strategies. They appreciate that there are thousands of brilliant investment plans and strategies available, BUT know that it takes a <u>DISCIPLINED investor to correctly execute them.</u> That is the Golden Key.

The share market statistics is a good example of the lack of DISCIPLINE & EMOTIONAL CONTROL people have when they invest in the share market as 80% of the people consistently lose money, 10% break even, and the remaining 10% consistently make money, these figures are frightening!

This is mainly due to people's lack of discipline in understanding their Trading Plan **thoroughly**, and their inability to follow their trading plan 110% of the time regardless of what they think, feel and/or the external influences they face.

<u>**The** share market exposes people's emotions, fear, greed and ego</u>. If you base your decisions on one of these emotions you will not succeed when investing in the share market.

Regardless of the investment vehicle you choose, you must follow the strategies within your Trading or Investment Plan and you must execute the strategies in a **non-emotional manner**. It is a concept that takes investors a while to grasp, as humans are naturally emotional about most decisions they make without realizing it.

The 10% who **consistently** succeed when investing in the share market are the investors who <u>do what is required</u> of them by understanding their investment plan and being disciplined enough to execute the necessary criteria without questioning if it is the right decision or not and whether it will work or not. This is known as **unconscious competence**.

So what is unconscious competence?

There are 4 stages of learning:

- *Unconscious* incompetence: This concept means that you have never tried a particular activity or it may be that you don't even know about the activity. If you have never ridden a horse, you would have no idea what it would feel like or what you would need to do.
- *Conscious* incompetence: Once you begin to learn to ride a horse you will quickly learn your boundaries and realise that you still have a lot to learn. You start to understand consciously how to interact with the horse on the ground; what motions or aids you need to give to the horse when riding to move forward, backwards, sideways, and at what pace you want to move.
- *Conscious* competence: You now know how to ride the horse but you have to concentrate very hard to get in tune with the horse. You understand the concept of horsemanship but haven't mastered it.
- *Unconscious competence:* You have finally learned to handle and move with the horse in unison. Both you and the horse understand that you are higher up in the order of the 'herd hierarchy' and that you are the leader; both understand the body language of the other and to carry out many different activities as one. Your interaction with the horse is on a subconscious level where you don't need to think about what you do next, your actions are very much

instinctive. Your conscious mind decides on the goal and your unconscious mind carries the command through.

Achieving the 4th level is the ultimate goal for any endeavour as you would have learnt how to respond automatically without having to think consciously of it.

How do you achieve unconscious competence?

Unconscious competence can only be achieved through **repetition**. Some people are predisposed to achieving unconscious competence quickly, as their upbringing was structured and disciplined, so they naturally take on new things with an ordered approach. They study all the details & fine print, crossing the "t's" and dotting the "i's". However, too much focus on the fine prints can sometimes prevent investors from executing investment transactions in a timely manner. So finding the right balance is what you are looking for, as you don't want to become obsessive with the detail that you never turn the key in the lock (metaphorically).

ACTION in the right areas is required and simplicity is important. We like to use the analogy of cooking as most people can relate to this. The tastiest recipes generally have the least amount of ingredients. Sometimes adding more strategies and tools to your investment plans sounds appealing but this can lead to over kill, so try to avoid the temptation. Use what works, and don't over complicate matters.

Seek knowledge before starting out; although there is a wealth of information available to you out there, you need unbiased and independent advice on what financial strategy suits you best. Seek a wealth mentor and/or a financial advisor to guide you in the right direction so that you can learn your chosen subject.

Learn the skills you require, attend free courses and training, gain as much experience as possible until you are satisfied that you have an understanding of what you want to achieve, and that the financial instrument chosen is in alignment with your lifestyle and financial goals.

Surplus Spender versus Deficit Spender

When you understand that your habits, self-image and level of awareness control your ability to be wealthy, you will be in a better position to handle the money that comes your way.

The Surplus or Deficit Spender is the habit that forms the foundation of whether someone is wealthy or poor. **The** issue is not how much you make, but how much you save/invest.

We know that many of you will be saying well if I made £500,000 a year, and spent the whole £500,000 a year on myself I will be much happier than what I am right now.

Unfortunately, this is not possible because whether you like it or not the tax man would take what is due to him, likewise your mortgage company/landlord and utility providers. You would also have failed to set aside funds for transport, travel and day to day expenses including emergencies which may occur.

IMPORTANT NOTE:

The key to knowing if you <u>truly</u>
understand something is if you have
successfully integrated it into your life. How
often do we hear ourselves and others say,

"Oh yes, I know that"

. . . but the key is, are you successfully
doing it?

<u>Knowing and doing are
very different.</u>

You can only fully understand something if you are successfully doing it. Not until you can successfully do something <u>consistently</u> will you really understand how to do it.

Stop and listen as this is a very important part of wealth building as it may take sometime for you to <u>truly understand and make the necessary changes to your current habits</u>. Each one of us falls under one of the following three categories—a Deficit Spender, a Break Even Spender or a Surplus Spender.

Deficit Spender	They spend more than they earn. (More money is going out than is coming in). Many fall into this category with today's credit problems.

Break Even	They spend only what they earn.
Surplus Spender	They save/invest more than they spend. This is what each of us needs to aim at in order to become wealthy and retain our wealth.

Obtaining & Retaining Wealth

Most people know the statistics of the lotto winners; the majority of winners are right back to where they started within 3 years. This is because they do not know how TO MANAGE THEIR MONEY. They obtained the money, but were unable to retain it.

As the majority of people fall within the DEFICIT thinking/ spending category, even though they now have MORE money, the conditioning of their subconscious mind is that of a deficit spender, so they simply buy more expensive things until the money is gone.

Have the resilience to work your way out of the debts that you have incurred. Get out of the worker/spender mentality. The deficit and the break even spenders will receive their pay check on a Friday, and cannot resist the temptation to spend their money until it is all gone. Stop purchasing items that depreciate in value and which gives you only temporary satisfaction, take a good stock of your debts and work towards clearing them.

Learn to take time to make financial decisions, ask for a cooling off period to carefully consider your options. That way you don't have to say yes immediately which will save you a lot of money in the long term as your decisions won't be based on emotional impulses.

So getting more money is not the solution. It is the **MANAGEMENT** of your money that will enable you to become and stay wealthy. No matter which way you look at it, if you want to increase your wealth, you will have to manage your money effectively and ideally increase your cash flow. But how do you do that when you have a job, a family and all sorts of other stuff going on in your life?

We know it's tough, but whichever way you look at it, you will dramatically speed up the process when you increase your cash flow. We want to share with you many ways of increasing and multiplying the little finances you have presently.

For most people, their primary source of income is of course their job . . . over time, you increase your cash flow but you can't avoid the temptation to spend more . . . And usually, it's with items such as bigger houses for the family, a more expensive car or perhaps a holiday or two and a stack load of depreciating household items.

But here's the problem. Your salary can increase from £25,000 a year to £50,000 a year and the reality is that you're not creating and retaining any wealth. If you are spending your money on depreciating household items, even though you just doubled your income, you wouldn't be able to dramatically change your lifestyle.

Once you've had a taste for a bigger house and a better car, you'll never ever want to step backwards again. You've locked yourself into your job for a very long time—if you like it, that's great. But if you don't, it's awful.

The answer is . . . . Do not rely on just a single source of income to attain financial freedom. What you need are Multiple Streams of Incomes (MSIs). Multiple Streams of Income is discussed in Chapter 3 of this book.

Wealth & Faith

"God's gift to you is more talent and ability than you could possibly use in your lifetime. Your gift to God is to develop as much of that

talent and ability as you can in this lifetime."
—Steve Bow.

There is a significant connection between your spiritual life and the 'right to be rich'. A great misunderstanding within many communities is that God somehow wants us to remain in poverty to show that we are humble.

God wants all individuals to live fully; experience life with the greatest happiness and with the ultimate expression of love. Unfortunately this expression of love is often frustrated and repressed by poverty. When people are struggling to pay their bills they quickly turn their irritations directly onto their loved ones, and their lives become a vicious circle of blame and hurt.

Depression and anger are most often the emotions built up by lack of funds. It is more selfish to remain in poverty than to be wealthy because you are not be able to contribute to or give anything back to the community in which you live, your family or to good causes. A person who has no money has very limited resources to help others.

When we create more wealth in our own lives we have more money to share with others and spend on ourselves. We can help build businesses, create jobs, find cures for diseases, save animals and contribute to researches etc.

Money itself is certainly not evil and should not be condemned. It creates order within our societies and needs to be appreciated for the power it brings when used wisely with the right attitude.

To our own detriment we have unfortunately assumed it is selfish and greedy to want anything more and that money is the cause and root of all evil. Some who live in poverty look at the wealthy and think they must have stolen their wealth from others to be rich; that they hoard their money and don't give to the needy; that they must be acting against the will of God; or simply purchasing luxury items to show off their wealth to belittle others.

People who are poor often think this way because they are either jealous of the rich or angry for being poor as they are unable to afford the luxuries of life which they crave. But what does God actually say? Do we actually understand His messages of wealth? It seems over time His messages have been lost in translation.

Your ability to create, increase and retain wealth is from God. God has ample untapped resources to meet your needs. Your diligence and respect for money would cause you to have wealth. Your honour and respect for God and humility before Him will open up doors of favour for you. God will give you the wisdom, knowledge, technical know-how and financial acumen to create wealth.

The treasures of God are for those who are just and right before Him. When God gives you wealth, it comes with joy, peace, happiness and contentment.

The Bible scriptures say the following;

1) *"But you shall [earnestly] remember the Lord your God, for it is He Who gives you power to get wealth, that He may establish His covenant which He swore to your fathers, as it is this day." Deuteronomy 8: 18 (Amplified)*

God is your source of wealth and not man, your physical prowess or mental acumen. God can cause your family or friends to leave an inheritance for you which you have not earned or worked for. You must never forget that it is God alone who has empowered you to create wealth.

Wealth is a blessing from God and He would cause opportunities to arise for you. When you become wealthy God expects you to utilise it for the benefit of others around you and to invest it wisely.

29

2) *"Keep on asking and it will be given you; keep on seeking and you will find; keep on knocking [reverently] and [the door] will be opened to you." Matthew 7:7 (Amplified)*

You must be very clear of WHAT you are asking for. Remember that true understanding of a concept can only be confirmed when you are successfully and consistently implementing the principles you have learnt from it. God will always give you what you are asking for. And what we are asking for is by and large what we spend most of our time thinking about, which is often money, wealth and freedom.

If you want wealth keep asking God for it as He would not deny you any good thing.

3) *"For as he thinks in his heart, so is he . . . (Proverbs 23:7 Amplified)*

Majority of people haven't really thought about what they 'think about', and are really in this negative loop where they continually worry over controversial issues within their lives.

We all know the saying "be careful what you wish for". So whether our time is spent thinking of positive things like wealth strategies, love, adventure, prosperity, good health and fitness or worrying about negative things like accidents, stress, disease, jealousy and poverty you will usually find yourself getting what you are thinking of.

If you spend most of your time thinking about what you desire **you** will receive it. The converse also holds true, if you spend more time and energy thinking (asking) for what you **do not** desire you will receive that.

People in poverty spend too much time thinking and reflecting on what they don't want. They fixate and preoccupy their time with the wrong things rather than utilising and implementing strategies that will enable them to achieve their desires and goals.

The acquisition of wealth requires great reflection and planning. Your current results are a direct reflection of your thoughts and your habits.

Wealth and Health

Can wealth really have an impact on your health? The answer is an affirmative yes.

Wealth is defined as having an abundance of valuable material possessions or resources. It is the state of being rich materially, socially, spiritually, physically and mentally. Wealth is linked to health, as the abundance of wealth affects your health positively.

Wealth is prosperity . . . Wealth is Health . . . and Health is Wealth.

The more affluent you become the more disposable income you have available to you to obtain the best health care protection in the market. Wealth allows you more recreation time; it allows you to set your working hours around yourself and the things you like.

When you are in a position to set your own working schedule, your stress level reduces which will have a positive impact on your family. Having an abundance of wealth will give you the opportunity to expand your assets and fulfil your dreams.

It can be argued that the converse is also true, your health impacts on your ability to create wealth. The healthier you are, the more time and energy you have to focus on wealth creation strategies. Can wealth bring you happiness, well the answer is relative as it depends on whether you positively or negatively utilise it.

"The first wealth is health"
—[Ralph Waldo Emerson (1803-1882),
U.S., essayist, poet, philosopher

When you are mentally and physically healthy you would make sound decisions and have the energy to act promptly. Having good health will hold you in good stead. **So look after your health by:-**

- Going for regular medical check ups
- Eating a healthy and balanced diet
- Exercising
- Having healthy relationships with other people around you
- Having sufficient sleep

Chapter 2

Money, Money, Money

What is Money?

We all know what money is in its physical form; money is simply described as either a piece of paper or metal. It is an item with an agreed value which is used as a medium of exchange for goods & services and in settlement of our debts. Money also serves as a standard value for measuring the comparative worth of various goods and services.

Money is a concept understood worldwide, we may not understand each other's language but we do understand the exchange and power of money across continents.

Without money economies would be extremely inefficient. During the time of the old Barter system problems frequently arose when traders were unable to reach an agreement of equal value for a commodity. A cow herder may want 10 chickens and only have a cow to exchange. The cow may be equal to 100 chickens. Therefore, the two farmers will need to find other items to make up the balance of the value of the cow. Money simplifies the agreement of value between traders.

The efficiency that economies gain through the use of money is the encouragement of trade and the divisions of labour, therefore increasing productivity and wealth of economies.

You working for MONEY

To increase cash flow, majority of the population have been brought up, or CONDITIONED to believe they need to work harder . . . just look at how many people are working over the standard 40 hours week, some are working in excess of 60-80 hours to increase their wealth. However having a (earning money per hour) working class mentality is the wrong belief system to have when you want to create wealth.

Working for money restricts your ability to see other opportunities that may come your way. This belief system only allows you to have two strategies which are 1) you must work more hours and/or 2) get a pay rise to make it in life. These strategies are very limited.

There are only 24 hours in a day; you can't work all of those 24 hours (on a continuous basis). A pay rise is also limited because a company will only pay you a salary in line with the need/value of your position and how much your position contributes to its business.

Money working for YOU

The concept of 'Money working for YOU' rather than 'YOU working for Money' is how the wealthy think and operate. They also only have 24 hours in a day, but they maximise these hours by LEVERAGING THEIR TIME and MONEY. By leveraging both your time and money you take the limits off your ability to create wealth.

Most people focus incorrectly on Income not Investments. Having your money work for you means you have invested your money into areas that can make you a **Passive Income (also known as 'Residual Income')**. This means that you are not swapping your time for money rather your money is making money for you, even while you sleep. When your money is at work for you, you don't even need to work up a sweat.

Some examples of money working for you, especially when you are asleep are:-

- Investing in real estate/property;
- Business ownership (where other people work for you and you have minimal, if any, involvement);
- Investing in the share market;
- Internet or network marketing etc . . .

(Strategies within these investment areas are found later in this book).

We can hear many of you say, 'I don't know a thing about these areas', or 'these investments are risky!' Well the biggest risk is staying where you currently are in your life. You either get educated or find someone who is successfully investing in these areas to do it for you. We are not saying everyone needs to go out and study these areas in depth, but what we are saying is that you need to at least understand the basics of money and its management.

If you have a PASSION TO CHANGE YOUR LIFE then you need to be aware that ACTION is very important to achieving the NEW RESULTS that you desire.

So many people want to achieve new results in their lives but they keep repeating the same actions they have been doing their whole lives. Get off the couch and create some new habits. Your first step is to read some of the recommended books and visit the web links mentioned at the end of this book.

Pay yourself FIRST before others!

The WEALTHY are well disciplined at paying themselves first before others, this is the wealth rule. The poor certainly do not follow or consider this cardinal rule.

- A person with a poverty mindset receives their income, pays their bills first, then their living expenses and then spends the rest.
- A person with a wealthy mindset pays God first (tithe and offering) as they understand that He is the source of their wealth, then themself, then their living expenses & bills last.

This does not mean that the wealthy don't pay their bills on time, they simply give MORE IMPORTANCE to paying themselves a minimum of 10% of everything they earn, which goes straight into solid investments (or at the minimum a savings account).

Multiply your Money: Compounding

When used properly money can become a very powerful tool.
We recommend the following book which teaches the principles
and power of compounding.
—"The Richest Man in Babylon" by George S.Clason

Albert Einstein is reputed to have said that compounding is the 8th wonder of the world. COMPOUNDING is the re-investment of the money you make from an investment. It means that you are reinvesting the money earned on your initial capital.

So if you invested £10,000 and obtained a 10% pa return year after year, and reinvested all these returns then you would have compounded your capital; **Year 1: £10,000 + 10% = £11,000, then with the growth after Year 2: £11,000 + 10% = £12,100, and so on until you get to £10,000 + 10 years compounding interest of 10% = £25,937.**

Well what if you were to step it up just a little more with an extra £1,000 savings each year? **£10,000 + £1,000 annually + 10 years compounding interest of 10% = £43,468.** Let's get a little more aggressive with a higher return of 15% pa and annual savings of

£2,000 – certainly workable for the average person. **£10,000 + £2,000 annually + 10 years compounding interest of 15% = £87,154**. Can you see how these little changes really affect your investment or savings in a huge way?

Saving Versus Investing

Another thing drummed into us by our parents and society is that we must save, save, save. Then we ask, "what for? " And the answer is "A rainy day" or "an "emergency".

Whilst saving is a good habit to get into, investing is a much more highly effective way of multiplying your money. So invest rather than save—preferably do both. Can you imagine what would have happened if your parents had told you to invest rather than save? You would probably be reaping the benefits right now.

The share market has outperformed every other investment vehicle over the last decade so by now you could be holding some bank shares worth 5 – 10 times more than what you paid for them rather than some miserly return you get from your savings account. Not only would you be receiving capital growth from your shares as they increase in value, but you would also be receiving a regular income from dividends which you would definitely re-invest.

Everyone should be taught to invest (or at least 'save') a minimum of 10% of their income. Now we are sure many people will be saying, "I can't afford to save or invest". **Well you cannot afford <u>not</u> to**. Even people not working who are on some form of income support or benefit should learn how to save/invest 10% of what they receive. People can become quite creative when pushed into a corner.

Think about it, you weren't always on the income you are on right now, and we know that your expenses were not as high either. You need to start following the strategies of the wealthy no matter what level you currently are at, otherwise you will never become financially free.

Managing Risk

You will often hear people say that investing is 'risky'. When people make statements along these lines, it is apparent that they have a limited knowledge of investments. Once you acquire financial knowledge you will recognize that risks can be managed, therefore investing can be quite safe as the risk can be predetermined and minimised by using the investment strategies and tools available in the market.

Informed investors only put money into investments with a sound and proven track record.

If the risk is too high they will not take on the investment as their No.1 goal is always to preserve their initial capital.

Risk management can come in various forms such as:-

- The investor knows his exact worst case scenario exit point prior to getting in, should the investment go against his favour. The decision is made in advance. There is no need to wonder and worry about when you will exit in the investment, the criteria is clearly pre-defined.
- The investor spreads his money across various investment types and strategies as he understands that there will be investments that will go wrong. When money is spread across different economies, asset classes and sectors it reduces the risk of over exposing his capital. Novice investors often make the mistake of putting all their eggs into one basket.
- Allocation of capital is important. Wise investors never over expose themselves by putting too much of their capital into too few investments, as one large loss could take out a significant component of their capital.

Chapter 3

The Streams of Income

Multiple Sources of Income (MSI)

If you like the concepts of a passive/residual income then let us tell you about Multiple Sources of Income (MSI). People with a poverty mindset tend to rely on a single source of income, namely their **'JOB'** (Just Over Broke) where payment is only via money per hour.

The WEALTHY however rely on **Multiple Sources of Income** and understand that although there may be a shortfall in one source of income that their other sources will provide cash flow and income for them. They have many streams of **passive** income that do not require much of their physical input as the income will be generating for itself. These MSI's come from investing in real estate/property, the share market, businesses, collectables, affiliate/network/internet marketing. Etc.

Many of the MSI's may initially take some time to set up or research into but they eventually require little or no effort in their returns in the form of capital growth, dividends, rental income and royalties.

A person having a poverty mindset goes from being employed to being self employed, but as Robert Kiyosaki states in his book "Rich Dad, Poor Dad" people who are self employed have simply created a job for themselves and should not consider their self employed businesses as an investment if the business relies on them being there always. A true business investment indicator is if the business still runs efficiently and profitably if you go away for six months. Most self-employed people can't do this because they know that their business relies heavily on them being there and would collapse without them.

Three Rules of a True Investment:

- It must bring in an income, (dividends, rental income, and/ or royalties).
- It must increase in value over time, (capital growth).
- It must be readily saleable to another person.

Obviously you wouldn't dismiss an investment or business proposition simply because it didn't fulfil all the criteria mentioned above; however these rules can be useful to you when you are making a decision as to which investment vehicle to choose from.

Diversification

Establishing Multiple Sources of Income is very much the same as Diversification. Diversification simply means that you are "spreading your risk" or "not having all your eggs in one basket" and it's a common risk management technique where investors mix a wider variety of investments in a portfolio. It is commonly practised in investments.

When investing in shares you can spread your risks across different sectors, asset classes, economies, mutual funds, currencies, commodities and stocks.

When investing in real estate/property you can spread your risks across residential housing, commercial properties, and land investments, holiday lets and properties in different countries.

All countries have downturns in their economies and industries, even locations have specific associated risks within themselves, so spreading your capital across an array of unrelated areas protects your portfolio from excessive downturns.

A word of caution, you must ensure that you do not diversify just for the sake of it. We do not want you to think that you are safe simply because you have spread your risks across different portfolios and hold on to non-performing investments. Do not keep your money in non-performing investments for the sake of it or because you have other high performing investments within your portfolio.

Opportunity Cost

There is something called **Opportunity Cost**. An opportunity cost is the cost of a missed opportunity. This occurs when you hold non-performing investments when your capital could be better placed elsewhere. Why diversify across non-performing investments when you can diversify across better performing ones. It is important to always have strategies within each investment vehicle that keeps you in the better performing investments and out of the non-performing ones.

An example of an opportunity cost within the **share market** occurs when investors take the **'Buy and Hold'** approach to investing. As their investment time frame is 'long term', during the medium to longer term down turns they miss the opportunity of putting their money into a company whose share prices keeps rising in the short term. They stubbornly hold on to an underperforming stock waiting for the returns to pick up in the longer term.

Informed investors who understand how to 'short trade' the share market do not need to look for other opportunities as they know how to profit from declining markets.

The Economic Cycle:

It is common knowledge that we all go through different paradigms/cycles individually and therefore collectively we create an 'economic cycle or economic clock. These cycles of fluctuations moves between periods of rapid growth (expansion and prosperity); to periods of relative idleness or decline (contraction, recession or economic slowdown).

It all relates to the principle of 'supply and demand'. Production is normally measured in terms of GDP (Gross Domestic Product), which means that if in any two successive periods the GDP is negative then the economy is said to be in a recession. High unemployment is typical in a recession as employers need to reduce staff when production levels fall, therefore incomes shrink; and with less money to spend, consumers demand less and reduce their consumption.

Governments assist the recovery from a recession by encouraging their residents to spend more (this is known as fiscal policy) and by managing their interest rates (known as monetary policy). By governments increasing their spending on projects, there will be increased employment opportunities and more money available in the economy for spending.

This diagram gives you an idea of how the economic cycle/clock starts and finishes, it is not fool proof but gives investors a rough idea of what may lie ahead;

Rising Interest Rates

Rising Property Values

Falling Share Prices

Rising Inflation

Falling Inflations

Rising Overseas Reserves

Falling Commodity Prices

Rising Commodity Prices

Falling Overseas Reserves

Rising Share Prices

Falling Property Values

Falling Interest Rates

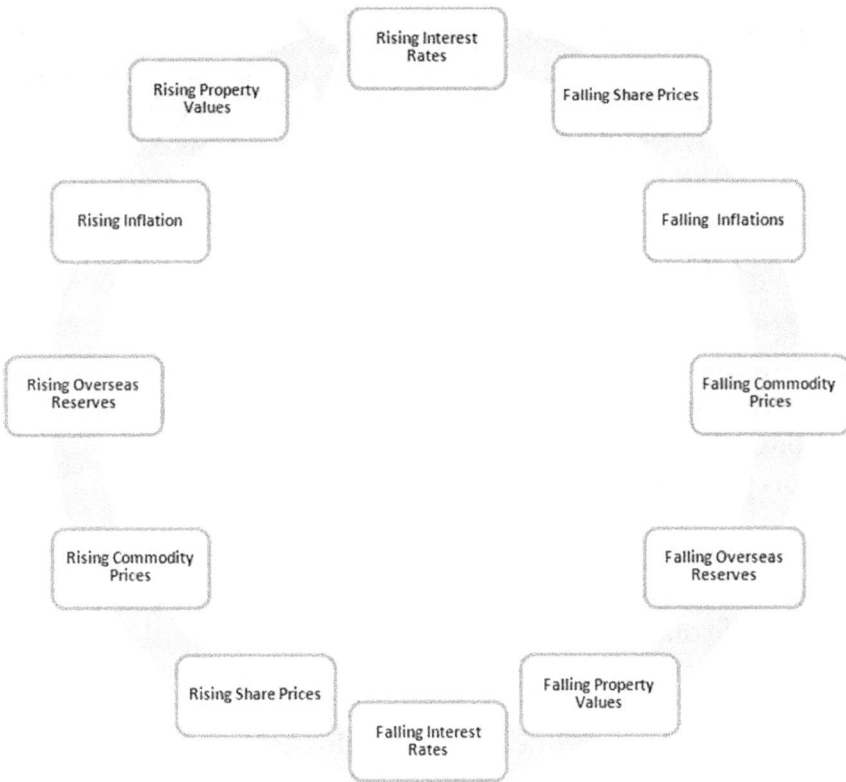

The Benefits of understanding The Economic Cycle

If an investor understands the different 'booms and busts' within the economic cycle/clock they can plan their strategies, time their diversification and maximise their returns.

The economic cycle can be likened to a clock; for example, you must seek to enter into the share market shortly after 6 o'clock once the recovery begins (this is where the 'smart investor' enters), and get out or 'short sell' around 12 o'clock to make a profit. Smart investors should aim to get out at the top of the economic cycle before the slump starts and then to re-enter and start the process again.

The period from 3-6 o'clock is where the economy slows down and productivity stalls and declines; at this point, there are fewer sales and a squeeze on earnings. As previously mentioned, if there are two consecutive periods where the GDP (Gross Domestic Product) is negative the economy is said to be in a recession.

The Global Financial Crisis (GFC) and the Age of Austerity

In many ways it may seem that the 'clock' described in the previous section has stopped! From the end of 2007 onwards the world's economies have suffered from the effect of the GFC and, at times, it seems like the crisis is never ending.

It is very useful to have an understanding of global economics and a handle on what is going on in managing your own personal finances. If you do then you will be better placed to make informed decisions that affect your wealth and develop strategies to help you weather the financial storms. Whilst this is not the place to cover the GFC in depth, a brief review at this point is useful. It will explain how we got to where we are now and, more importantly, what may happen in the future.

It is worthwhile understanding that the roots of the GFC came from a series of related developments in the world of economics and finance. Firstly, from the mid-1980's onwards, the financial world became more interconnected. Prior to this banking was more local, there were barriers stopping cross border trading. These were removed which opened the globe up to more sources of finance which drove down prices and increased competition. It also, of course, meant that the whole world was more susceptible to financial shocks.

Secondly, the cost of finance was further driven down by the expansions of global trade, the rise of global wealth and the general conquering of inflation. Apart from a few isolated shocks (the bursting of the dot com bubble and 9/11) the 1990's – 2007 was a golden period of economic growth with little inflation. Interest rates dropped, debt in all forms (credit cards, personal loans, mortgages etc.) was widely available and looked very cheap, and financial institutions fell over themselves to lend.

The third big change was that the world of finance got ever more complex. Some very clever people developed ways of packaging all this debt and selling it on to investors, making funding for future loans even cheaper. The big problem was that, as these instruments got ever more complex, fewer people understood them or the level of risk that was involved in them.

The result of all this was an explosion of debt. Debt is not necessarily a bad thing as long as a) markets/incomes are growing and b) the debt can be serviced. The problem was that financial institutions increased their market share by lending to people with very poor credit records (e.g. sub-prime mortgages) with very poor security checks to determine whether they could actually pay the loans back, and then bundled up these loans and sold them onto other financial institutions as prime stock.

But that wasn't all; the debt problem applied at country levels too.

The expansion of the European Union and the launch of the Euro brought a number of countries which had questionable economic records (Greece, Ireland, Portugal and Spain for example) into a system where suddenly they had access to interest rates that were greatly lower than they had been able to achieve alone. Not surprisingly they borrowed to fund their now booming economies, although many of these countries had poor records in terms of things like public spending (high) and taxation collection (low) and therefore had little real prospect of repaying the debt if things turned sour. Even larger, more well managed economies, like the

UK, borrowed excessively in this time of easy credit and low interest rates.

The crunch came when defaults started on those US sub-prime mortgages. Suddenly those financial institutions with the bundles of debt realised that they had not bought prime stock but pure junk. There was a crisis of confidence that spread throughout the financial world; the fire started in the US but spread rapidly to European banks and building societies (e.g. RBS and Northern Rock), who stopped lending to each other, and then the scrutiny fell onto countries and their ability to service loans – and the rest is history.

This is why the world in general is in such a difficult position. The easy access to cheap finance which fuelled growth has gone. It is why the position in Europe is so difficult; it was quickly realised that countries like Greece and Ireland had no real ways of paying back their mountain of debt. The only solution for these countries was to cut back severely on expenditure (hence the public sector job cuts, the slashing of benefits and pensions) and attempts to increase revenue (tax increases and the selling off of public assets). Even then interest rates to these countries rose, making the situation even worse.

Although the UK is outside the Euro Zone, the UK was always going to be badly affected. Firstly, as an EU member, the UK's major export markets are in Europe. Whilst the severe austerity measures have dampened future growth in the region the UK's own growth has been restricted. Secondly, the UK's own debt had skyrocketed and needed to be reduced. Whenever the global financial community became doubtful about a country's financial viability then interest rates on loans to that country skyrocketed (hence UK's struggle to regain its high credit rating, the triple A that it has lost).

So this is where we are, all of Europe trying to balance the need for growth whilst controlling debt. It is a very tricky balancing act.

So what does this mean for your own personal wealth?

Recession Strategies—for personal GFCs

Most of these strategies depend on your personal circumstances. **You may well be facing your own mini—GFC** with high levels of debt and reduced income. In these circumstances the best strategy is often similar to those followed by many countries; you have to do everything you can to reduce your debt (or at least reduce the servicing cost of your debts by either consolidating it or switching to the lowest cost source; unsecured loans like credit cards have a high interest rate whilst secured forms such as approved overdrafts and mortgages are much cheaper. It is always better to increase a mortgage than increase your credit card balance) whilst doing everything to maximise your income.

The worst thing you can do – as countries have found out – is to increase your debt in the hope that things will improve in the future.

There are also crucial things to be aware of:

1. Beware of exchange rates moving against you. One thing that the UK has done to make its exports cheaper and boost its economy is to allow exchange rates to slip against the rest of the world. The unfortunate thing is, if you are lucky enough to own assets like a holiday property abroad, the value of your overseas income will have fallen.
2. Beware of interest rate rises. The Government and the Bank of England have held interest rates at a historic low level for many years to encourage the economy. At some point, oddly enough when the economy improves, the interest rates WILL rise, and rise quite a lot. Although the current low rates offer opportunities if you are in a position to take advantage of them (funding buy-to-let property purchases for example), a wise investor will look

carefully at the position they will be in when interest rates return to their normal levels. What these 'normal' levels will be depends on a number of factors, particularly the level of growth and inflation in the economy, but most people feel that a long term base rate of between 4%-6% is most likely.

So is everything black in this new austere economy? Well, no, there are still investments that do well in a recession plus there are a number of business/employment opportunities that these conditions have opened up.

The two best investment opportunities are:

(a) Gold/Precious Metals. One of the two investments that always do well in a recession is gold/precious metals. Investors always return to these solid sources of wealth in times of financial uncertainty.
(b) Rental Property also does well in downturns – as people either lose their homes or are priced out of the home-owning market by income or credit restrictions, so rental property tends to boom. This has implications for employment business opportunities as well, which will be discussed below.

The business/employment opportunities that are opened up by a recession are as follows:

(i) Re-sale shops – either virtual (e.g. eBay) or real (e.g. cash-converters) do really well as people look to release their cash from the things they have bought in better times.
(ii) Repair businesses – In recession's people make do and mend rather than buy new. Businesses and employment connected with repairing things like cars, computers, jewellery and houses do really well.

(iii) Property letting and Management – As rental properties increase so the demand for people to manage them increases. The one growth area in Estate Agency businesses in recent years have been residential lettings. There is also a huge demand for maintenance and management businesses.

(iv) Temping and Freelancing – In recessions companies lay off staff to reduce costs and are reluctant to rehire on a long-term basis. This has led to a boom in temporary work and freelancing. Do you have skills that can be used in this way? If so you can often charge a premium for them. You may consider running an agency that meet companies' needs in times of recession.

(v) Outsourcing generally – This is very much connected with the last point. Companies in recent years have looked to outsourcing a lot of functions that they would normally have kept in-house-everything from payroll to PR. Companies or individuals that can provide these functions are in much demand.

(vi) Cost Reduction businesses – Companies and individuals are always seeking ways of reducing costs. There is one particular field where this is increasingly true; energy. Energy costs have risen hugely; as resources run down they would have to be replenished. There is now the need to move to low-carbon technology. There are a number of companies doing good business by negotiating low carbon technology contracts on behalf of their corporate clients with suppliers. The field of energy conservation and green energy alternatives are big growth areas.

The current economic climate can be depressing; however the more you understand about how the economy works the better you will be at predicting the future.

Franchising

One way of expanding your income stream is by buying a franchise.

Franchising is a popular term that is frequently tossed about. It is also an increasingly popular route, particularly for those making the transition from employment to being self-employed; for, in some ways, operating a franchise is like being self-employed but with a safety net.

So what is franchising?

A franchise basically is where you buy the rights to replicate the franchisor's business, including using their branding and business model. This is usually within a defined territory, although some franchises allow you to trade internationally. The purchase normally involves an outright fee and then, usually, an on-going franchise charge paid monthly, quarterly or annually. Sometimes there is a requirement for a share of profit or turnover to be paid as well. In return you get the franchise model, the branding, the territory rights, training and support.

This sounds good to many people; you are getting a proven business model and the freedom that working for yourself gives – and, when it works well, franchising can be very successful for everyone involved. There are pitfalls, however, and like every activity, you should go into franchising with your eyes open.

Let us have a quick look at some of the disadvantages of franchising so you are aware of the pitfalls before being drawn further into the idea by the many potential advantages.

Disadvantages of Franchising

1. Expense – Franchising can be an expensive way of setting up in business, swallowing up often high capital costs before

you start. We will see some of the costs below, but note that it can take a while to start recouping these costs.

2. Lack of Flexibility – One of the joys of being your own boss is the freedom and flexibility it offers you. Often you do NOT get this with franchising; you have to operate the business according to the model you are given by the franchisor. This is understandable; it is their brand image that you are representing and any variation from the service model may reflect badly on them; however it may make the franchisee feel like a glorified employee who has actually paid for the privilege of working for the company;

3. Fraud—You may become a victim of shady operators as there is no specific legislation dealing with who can set up a franchise. There are some people who have set up franchise businesses which have no real prospect of earning a living for the franchisees – essentially that is the way the parent business makes its money. This became such a concern that questions were asked in the House of Commons in the UK (though the UK Government declined to act). The only solution to avoiding this is to carry out proper investigations beforehand (see below).

There is some self-regulation through the British Franchise Association (BFA) and the UK Franchise Organisation. If you deal with members of these organisations you at least have some assurance about their genuineness. Memberships of these organisations are however expensive and there are some good operators who keep their costs down by not joining them – essentially it a case of being very careful with whom you deal with. There are also similar Associations and Organisations in other countries, they can be found on the internet.

Given the above, let us now look at some of the advantages of franchising.

Advantages of Franchising

There are lots of advantages of franchising. Some of these are:

1. You are self-employed, but have the support of the franchisor behind you. Often their profits depend on you being a success; therefore they will have a vested interest in supporting you.
2. You are operating a business model that has been tested, therefore it has more chance of succeeding than a cold start – there is therefore less risk.
3. You can get up and run quicker as the whole start up process is documented and you can refer to this as your guide.
4. Banks are usually more willing to lend start-up funds if you are operating a recognised franchise.
5. The franchisor will often help you with things like accounts and taxes – a major learning curve for most people starting a small business.
6. The success rate for franchise business is much higher than for other business start-ups.
7. The franchise business, once set up, can usually be resold at a higher value than the start-up cost

What are the leading franchises and what will they cost?

It is hard to be definitive about what the leading franchises are; it varies from year to year AND is very dependent on what your budget is; franchises vary from a few hundred pounds for online businesses or charity sweet distribution to several million pounds for something like McDonalds – yes, the golden arches operate a franchise model.

There are a number of franchising magazines, websites and Trade Bodies' materials detailing what franchises are available and the popular ones. Some of these magazines, websites and Trade Bodies can be found at the following web links:

http://www.franchise.org/
http://www.thebfa.org/
http://ukfo.org/
https://www.franchiseinfo.co.uk/
http://www.thefranchisemagazine.net/
http://www.theukfranchisedirectory.net

To give an idea of the range of the initial investment required at the time of writing (2013), the following list has been created:

Low Cost Franchises (0-£10,000 initial costs)

- Web Based Magazines – e.g. About My Area,
- Charity Sweets Distribution
- Low Cost Vending
- Internet travel agencies

Low/Medium Franchises (£10,000—£50,000 initial costs)

- B2B type operations – e.g. Agency Express Signs Business
- Employment Type Agencies co-ordinating workers – e.g. Bluebird Care
- Shops – e.g. Cash Generators
- Van based maintenance systems—MetroRod Home maintenance

Medium Costs (£50,000-£250,000)

- Bigger Retail Outlets – e.g. Cash Converter Outlet
- National entry level food businesses – e.g. A Subway Outlet

High Costs (£250,000 plus)

- Internationally known hot food businesses/ retailers—McDonalds

Which franchise should you choose?

Not every franchise is suitable for everyone, but the range of franchises that are available mean that you will almost certainly find a franchise that is suitable for you! For example, if you like being outdoors there are a number of lawn care franchises. If you are good with your hands, there are a number of car based systems such as Chips Away. If you like pets, there are dog grooming businesses. Similarly there are opportunities in education, computing and website design, photography, retailing and business-to-business (B2B) operations.

So how do you choose?

If you want to own a successful franchise it is important that you do something that firstly interests you and secondly that you can do!

Firstly, do plenty of looking around. Visit the websites, get the literature, and perhaps go to a franchising show (see the above websites for details). This should enable you to settle on a shortlist of opportunities that you would feel comfortable doing and, importantly, you can afford.

You may need to talk to your bank at this point if you need funds to buy the franchise. Sound them out about their attitude to lending to you.

Once you have done this then investigate these industries carefully. Are they growing areas or is the business sector saturated. It is alright for a business to have a territory available in your area but what are the competitions doing? Are there other franchise businesses operating in your area? If so, how many are they? Is there enough business for you to obtain?

If you are then satisfied there are two important meetings (or, at worst, long phone calls) to have.

The first is with the franchisor. Talk to them; see what they have to offer. Look at how they operate. What kind of people are they? Do you think you can work with them? Do not be afraid to ask awkward questions; listen carefully to the answers. Preferably this meeting should be at their head office; if not ask to visit it in the future. You want to be certain that they have the resources that they say they have. Remember if the parent company goes under you will have lost your franchise fee. It is important that you do not sign up at this point.

The second is to have a meeting with/speak to existing franchisees. Ask for a list and the freedom to talk to who you like. Speaking to existing franchise owners – and not just the 'stars' – will give you an idea of what it is really like to work as a franchisee within the organisation of your choice.

Finally, do some internet research looking for bad press about the franchise. You will have to be sensible about this, some industries always generate bad press – McDonalds for example; it doesn't make them a bad company but rather an easy target! What you are looking for is a stream of complaints from customers and other franchise holders. If you find it, walk away!

The Franchise Agreement

One final thing to remember about franchising is that you will be signing a franchise agreement. This is a legally binding document and, as such, should be checked over carefully to see what your rights and responsibilities are. This will include what you have to pay and when. Be careful with this document; if in doubt seek legal advice.

In conclusion, although there are pitfalls, franchising is the answer to many people who want to work for themselves but do not want to go out on a limb and start something new. Franchising is so varied that there is something for almost everyone – there are even part time franchises that can be run whilst continuing to work full time – this is a popular choice for people wanting to achieve financial freedom. Be aware though; the most successful franchises are almost invariably the most expensive. You get what you pay for. But there are opportunities still out there, particularly with new franchised industries that you may need to take a risk on to be in at the beginning.

Be flexible and open – but be careful!

Real Estate Investing

Bricks and mortar is the most common form of investment. It is attractive because it is tangible; it is also easier to obtain finance on property than any other form of investments; and it is almost inflation proof.

Many people incorrectly see their own home as an investment and unless they are receiving an income from it, it is usually costing them in the form of interest rates, mortgage payments, council rates and maintenance. The power in real estate investing comes from accumulating properties within a Portfolio that provide you with capital growth, rental returns and tax offsets.

Accessing equity from the capital growth within your home is a great way of funding deposits for more rental properties and growing a property portfolio. Ensure you do not over expose yourself and that you can afford to service any or all of the loans should you find the property/ies unoccupied for some time.

Buffers or savings need to be factored in for periods of voids. So always focus on increasing your cash flow, either by getting a raise, another income, or preferably entrepreneurial methods like Multiple Sources of Income.

There are many strategies within real estate investing, such as:-

Buy and Hold Property Investing: It is essential that you purchase ALL your properties at Below Market Value (BML) as you make your money when you BUY and not when you sell. It is important to remember that the buy and hold strategy is a long term strategy;

you must buy when the prices are low and sell when the price is high. If you follow this rule then there is capacity for larger and quicker capital growth.

If you purchase a property following a period of significant capital growth then you run the risk of having a property which does not increase in value or the increase is minimal, so timing and good value for money is crucial. Buying a property under its market value is important as you never want to be caught out buying just before a downturn in the market only to find that your property is worth less than the loan you owe. This happens to many people who get caught up in the hype and buy too late into the economic cycle.

Momentum Property Investing: This strategy again requires you to buy the properties 'cheap'. The difference is that your intention is to sell the property quickly at a higher price for a quick profit. It is an aggressive strategy where you trade properties regularly to produce an income. Properties are usually snapped up when desperate vendors sell at a price below its value. The aim is to resell the property quickly enough to avoid the associated ongoing costs.

"Off Plan": is where you purchase properties often at a large discount from property developers during the building process or even before the foundation has been laid. Some informed property investors will purchase these properties "off plan" from developers and then resell them before the property project has been completed, or immediately the property is built for a tidy quick profit.

Other investors who do not sell the property up front tend to keep the property for sometime and rent it out. They re-finance or re-mortgage after they have completed the purchase and use the proceeds to finance the purchase of other properties.

You are always advised to include a "Sale on clause" before exchanging contract so that you can have the benefit of either completing the purchase with the developers or selling on to someone else without incurring a penalty or associated breach of contract fees/ litigation costs.

Land investments: This is another strategy used to increase your investment portfolio. Here the investor purchases a piece of land with the aim of holding on to the land for some years and then selling it on for a huge profit when the value has risen.

You must however be weary of scrupulous land developers who may wish to sell you land which is likely to depreciate because it is either contaminated or the government is unlikely to grant planning permission for the use intended. You must carry out your due diligence (enquiries) to ascertain whether any previous planning applications have been made and rejected.

Property letting/But to let: this is a form of property investment where investors buy a residential property to let out to tenants and become the landlord. Investors usually fund the purchase with the help of a mortgage (where the deposit required from the investor is around 20% of the purchase price as of April 2013).

This form of investment often requires a lot of input from the investor if he decides to manage the property himself. He would be responsible for sourcing tenants, checking their references, collecting rent and dealing with day to day issues that may arise.

As the landlord of the property, the investor would be responsible for the purchasing and replacing of fixture and furnishings when they wear and tear; ensuring annual gas and electrical safety certificates are obtained and carrying out both major and minor repairs to the property when damage occurs.

If the investor chooses to use the services of a management company, the management company would expect to receive anything between 10-20% of the rental income for carrying out the above mentioned duties and responsibilities. The decision as to whether or not the investor manages the property himself or through a management company is determined by whether or not the investor has the time and knowledge to do it himself.

Where the investor has a number of properties spread over the country or in different countries the best course of action is to use the services of a management company situated where the property is located, as the investor cannot be everywhere at the same time.

Commercial Properties: offices, shops and business complexes have the potential to provide higher rates of return on capital and have higher yields (rent). The tenants of commercial properties are more likely to be professionals like solicitors, accountants and employment agencies who tend to take longer leases (usually 5-10 years) thereby ensuring continuity of occupation and rental income.

This form of investment often requires less input from the investor as the tenant is often responsible for repairs and furnishings and the investor often uses the services of a management company situated where the property is located.

This form of investment however requires a larger deposit (usually around 30% of the purchase price as of April 2013) at the time of purchase and there are larger hidden costs. For the investor who is just starting out, this form of investment might prove to be too daunting as he/she does not know what the commercial market entails.

Holiday Lettings: Holiday Lets are properties which are rented out fully furnished by an investor to holiday makers for a certain number of days in the year. The holidaymaker pays in advance for renting the property and there is usually a tenancy agreement between the Landlord (investor) and the holiday maker. The investor is allowed to use the property during the vacant periods.

Each country has its own rules and regulations governing the operation and running of holiday lets. There are often guidelines as to the number of days the property must be made available to the public in the year, the type of furnishings and the rates (rents) charged by the investor.

Holiday lets is a new trend in the market both in the United Kingdom and overseas. In the UK, the government will treat such properties especially where they are furnished as business assets and will impose a different tax regime from other sources of rental income.

Before investing in this type of property, you must ensure that you understand the legal, financial and tax regimes operating in the country you are seeking to invest in, so that you do not fall foul of the law.

Holiday let properties could be a room in a hotel, a flat in a holiday resort, an apartment, house or a second home of the investor.

Property Investment Funds (PIF): If an investor wants to add properties to their Portfolio but do not have the time or the desire to do it themselves then an option is to invest in Property Investment Funds.

Investors can quickly and easily get involved in property investing and create leverage by using professional, experienced and proficient fund and property managers by pooling money with other investors in a fund, with a minimum contribution of £5,000, (more is preferable).

The pooled money is then geared with bank funding. Investors can diversify into various types of properties in different markets without the need to find property, hot spots, tenants, tradesmen or find deals themselves.

Time Share: buying into a time-share at your favourite holiday location is another way of increasing your property portfolio. These properties enable each owner to use the asset at different scheduled times throughout the year. Everyone shares the costs of running the resort/property. This strategy has been successfully applied to houseboats, yachts, camping grounds, caravans, private jets etc.

Irrespective of the property strategy chosen, you must consider Negative and Positive Gearing.

Negative gearing simply means that the renal income does not cover the loan repayment and associated letting/rental costs therefore you would have to make up the balance from your savings; whilst a positively geared property means you are receiving rental income above the repayments on the loan and cost of the letting/renting the property, and therefore you are making a profit.

Gearing is crucial as it affects cash flow; negative gearing eats away at the cash you have set aside for emergencies and ultimately leads to stress when you can't balance your books/accounts.

Rental Guarantees

Income flow from your property is crucial. You need a constant flow of income to meet your necessary operating costs and to obtain the maximum return on your investment. Rental Guarantee gives you peace of mind as it covers you against loss of rent; property damage, nuisance and trespass and it provides the cost of repossessing your property where the tenant refuses to pay rent and/or leave the premises at the end of their tenancy.

Commercial properties:

If you are dissatisfied with the covenant strength of your tenant, you can protect your asset by doing any of the following four things:

1. By requiring the tenant to place a bond on deposit in trust in an agreed bank. This should be for an agreed sum representing a period of rent (e.g. a quarter's rent, six months or one year)
2. By requiring the tenant to place a sum equivalent to the length of rent payment being guaranteed somewhere where you, as landlord, can access it if the tenant defaults. In an ideal world, you as landlord should not hold the deposit. It should ideally be held in an account operated by your solicitor to reassure the tenant that the funds are not going to be misused
3. By obtaining a rental guarantee from a parent company written into the lease (or a personal guarantee in the case of a newly formed or small limited company from a director)
4. By taking out a rental guarantee insurance, though this can be an expensive option, the cost of the premium can often be passed onto the tenant as a lease obligation

Note, with a good quality tenant it is unlikely that you will get acceptance for any of the above and insistence on these will probably cause the tenant to walk away from the property. In poor market conditions, when tenants are hard to find, a landlord will also have limited ability to impose clauses like these.

Residential lettings:

It should be noted that more regulations exist for this category. In the UK, for example, Rent deposits for residential premises are now protected by regulations. A landlord must join a Tenancy Deposit Scheme and failure to comply with the regulations entitles the tenant to sue for compensation equal to three times the value of the rent deposited.

There are five different approved Rental Deposit providers in the UK, these Government-backed schemes ensure that the tenant will get their deposit back if they:

- meet the terms of the tenancy agreement
- don't damage the property
- pay the rent and bills

You or your letting agent must put your deposit in the scheme within 30 days of getting it.

There are a number of companies offering Rent Guarantee insurance – it will pay to shop around if you want this security. In addition, some letting agencies will offer their own rental guarantee as an incentive for taking them on as managing agents for your properties, the agents picking up the bill for the months that a property is vacant. You should remember, however, that the cost of this will be factored into their management fee and this will only tend to be offered in very buoyant markets with high tenant demand.

Property Costs:

Make sure that you do your home work well as there are many costs involved with the purchase and selling of a property. Significant time is involved in buying and selling properties which needs to be considered and factored into your timescale.

Some hidden costs which many property buyers overlook or underestimate are:-

- *Purchase* costs: legal expenses, inspection expenses, loan expenses and government fees.
- *Inclusion* costs: ensure you budget a bit extra to ensure that you cover those extra expenses like curtains, lamp shades etc. As a rule of thumb allow 10% of the purchase price for a brand new home, and 3% of the purchase price for an established home.
- *Welcome* costs: these costs are those 'new' problems that spring up as soon as the property changes ownership. Such

as the water heater blowing up, leaking taps, cracks or blocks in sewer pipes etc.
- *Running* costs: on averages homes cost approximately an extra £75 per week in running costs, costs such as insurance, rates, maintenance etc, which can amount to as much as £4,000 per year! Ensure you allow for these extra costs when buying a property.

Key Pointers—Things to Note when letting a Residential Property

Remember to ask your mortgage company for permission to let your property. Not all mortgages allow letting (Buy-to-let ones do). They may want to see a copy of the Tenancy Agreement and may require you to take out insurance. Insurance is a sensible option in any event. The minimum you will need is Building Insurance; this will cover you for the replacement of the building should it be destroyed or become uninhabitable. The insurance company will need to know if the building is tenanted as the risks are often perceived as greater than those they are insuring when you apply for cover for your own home.

Whether you take out contents insurance often depends upon whether you let it as furnished or unfurnished. Do you have considerable value in the furnishings? If so, contents insurance may be wise.

If you are letting the property on an unfurnished basis, be aware that most tenants will require a cooker, refrigerator, carpets and curtains. If you are letting furnished, check that any furniture staying in the property complies with the Furniture and Furnishings (Fire) (Safety) Regulations 1988 or other applicable legislation where the property is situated.

To ensure that your property complies with all safety regulations you will need to book the following engineers before the start of the tenancy (some estate agents will do this for you):

- A Gas Safe registered engineer to assess the safety of all gas appliances. (Required by law £70.00 + vat)
- A qualified engineer to carry out a Portable Appliance Test (PAT) to assess the safety of all electrical appliances.

You are legally bound to obtain up-to-date service certificates on all gas and electrical appliances. Make sure the gas appliances are serviced by a CORGI approved contractor or other equivalent contractor where the property is situated.

If you're letting an apartment, make sure you let your management company know what you are doing.

Building a Property Portfolio

1. **Plan** of Action: First of all you need to have a vision of where you want to go and have a plan of how you intend to get there, (see goal setting exercise at the end of this book); which areas do you prefer to invest in within the property market? Is it residential (higher luxury end or middle class) or commercial properties? Which countries will you be investing in? How long do you intend to hold the properties for? Will you invest by yourself or with a group of others?

2. **Time** Frames: Set yourself realistic time frames to go with your goals otherwise you will feel deflated if you don't achieve your goals and may want to give up when things are not working.

3. **Increase** your cash flow: Always look for opportunities to increase your cash flow by setting up MSIs (Multiple Sources of Income), this will ensure you can cover the loan

repayments and insurance if there are periods of voids (no tenants).

4. **Protection** is essential: Insurance should always be kept up to date, (Home insurance and Public Liability). Use the services of a good broker who compares premium rates of various providers to ensure that you are getting the best rate for your money. Do not over or under insure yourself.

5. **Regimes**: Buying your first investment property may feel overwhelming as there are so many regimes (legal, financial and taxation) you need to look into. Ensure you seek the advice of professionals in these areas so that you do not breach the law or incur financial loss.

Also enlist quality professionals to review your contracts and to conduct inspections of your properties periodically. Remember not to fall in love with your investment properties as decisions need to be made without emotion.

Remember that you make your money when you BUY the property so if the figures don't stack up; walk away as there will be another more profitable deal around the corner. Don't be afraid to make a ridiculous offer, you may be surprised that your offer is accepted. People sell properties for many different reasons; you may never know why your seller is trying to get rid of his property. Always get detailed information about the property you want to buy.

6. **Rent** out your investment property: Getting tenants in as soon as possible is crucial so that the rent substitutes your loan repayments, and minimises your tax obligations.

7. **Economic** cycle: If you buy your first property at a good price, and at a good time during the economic cycle, you can quickly build up your equity and then borrow against

the equity to finance another property (second). This is the start of your property portfolio.

Buying properties below the market value (BMV) may require you buying properties that need cosmetic improvements to it. (If you are a handy man/woman this is advantageous, but remember that renovation or cosmetic improvements may take twice the length of time and money budgeted for, so ensure you can afford the extra work that is required.

8. ***Repeat*** the process: Ensure your formula can be duplicated so that once equity is built up in your 2nd property you can move on to purchasing your 3rd property. Once you get into the swing of things, the process becomes much easier. As you progress you will also find that you are building a great team of professionals (lawyers, estate agents, plumbers, electricians etc) who will assist you in achieving your goals in building a property portfolio.

How to raise a deposit for a property

1. Savings—using money sitting in your savings account;
2. Using equity from other properties;
3. Selling assets;
4. Borrowing it – from friends and family or by using your credit cards, but you must be disciplined enough to pay off your credit card debt as soon as the property is refinanced, sold or you come into some money;
5. Doing extra work;
6. Getting a guarantor;
7. Jumble sale of items you don't need which are piled up in your garage/store;
8. Buying jointly with someone;
9. Re-valuing and re-financing existing properties.

Where to find properties to buy

1. Developers—at discounts;
2. Auctions—check various auction websites /make phone calls to auctioneers for proposed property sale;
3. Newspaper advertisements;
4. Local Estate Agents/Realtors where the property is situated;
5. Word of mouth ;
6. Internet.

Due diligence—Questions to ask yourself before deciding whether or not to purchase a particular property

1. ***Condition*** of the property : Is the property brand new, old or dilapidated—does it need major work or just cosmetic improvements and what is the total cost of improvements/ repair if any;

2. ***Reasons*** for buying the property: Do you intend to buy and sell it quickly to make a quick profit or do you intend to let it out;

3. ***Buy*** to let: If you intend to let it, what is the likely rental income, what are the service rates, is the property in an area where people are likely to rent it or is it in an owner occupier area? Are there any amenities near the property such as schools, shops, trains and hospital etc?—these factors have an impact on the demand for your property;

4. ***Saleability***: If you are going to sell immediately after purchase for a quick profit what is the demand like for your property type—does demand exceed supply?

5. ***Financing***: Have you approached your broker, bank or mortgage company to arrange financing for the property?

have you obtained an agreement in principle –ensure that you have sought independent financial advice before selecting any product;

6. **Re-financing**: Are you able to re-finance your property soon after purchase to release some equity? Have you informed your broker /independent financial adviser of this?

Buy to let properties /Commercial lettings

When purchasing buy to let properties, you also need to consider the following:-

1. **Vetting** of potential tenants: Who would be responsible for vetting potential tenants? Would that be an Agent or yourself? How would you check potential tenants' references, credit ratings, previous addresses (3-5 yrs) and problems with previous landlords?

2. **Inspection** of property: Who would inspect the property? Would the inspection be carried out quarterly, six monthly? If there are damages to the property, how are they reported and who pays for them.

3. **Payment** of rent: Have direct debit arrangements been set in place for rent to be paid by the tenant each month to avoid late payment? What happens in the event of non payment or late payment of rent? What do you do with the deposit received? Do you or your Agent hold unto this? Have you also considered what the legal requirements are regarding holding of deposits in the country/state where the property is situated?

4. **Renewal** of tenancies: What is the procedure for renewing the tenancy? These must be stated clearly in the tenancy agreement to avoid any misunderstanding.

5. *Rental* Increase: How often do you increase the rent and by what percentage annually? Usually this is 4-6 % per annum for residential properties.

You must understand that it is up to you to decide what type of real estate strategy you choose to implement, no one can make the decision for you.

Are Buy-to-Let (BTL) Investments a Good Alternative to a Pension?

There is no easy answer to this one.

There is no doubt that, in the recent past, the performance of BTL properties have outstripped the returns on many of the traditional investment mediums that are typical of many pensions, however there have also been times when investment in property has looked extremely shaky. The future prospects for BTL property is mixed; on one hand, demand for rental property looks like it will continue to be high as people struggle to get on the housing ladder. On the other, after the global financial crisis it is unlikely that lending to the sector will be on such advantageous terms as in the past; interest rates will also almost certainly return to a higher level. All of these factors will tend to depress property values.

However, there is no doubt though that property investments remains a good path to wealth if it is done well. But it is a business that has to be actively managed to get the best out of it.

This makes it very different from a typical pension. With a pension you tend to pass on the management time and expertise onto specialist professionals. They sell their products to you on the evidence of their abilities measured in the returns they can offer. They also have the ability and financial muscle to switch the collective funds they manage into the most advantageous investments. This is quite different from property, which is a long

71

term investment with a low level of ability to switch funds in and out (as property tends to take a long time to sell).

Whether BTL is a viable alternative to pension depends very much on you as an individual. The potential returns are there (though there are risks) but only when managed as an active business. Do you have the time to do this? Or would you rather be doing something else whilst you let experts manage your pension fund? Are you willing to have substantial assets tied up in a property? Or are you happier spreading your risk in other forms of investments?

The final decision should be considered very carefully.

Share Market Investing

Share market investing is simply investing in the share market. Investment property is fantastic, especially when purchased at below market value (BMV) as huge profits can be made, however it is the share market that has an unlimited potential to meet any type of financial and lifestyle goals you may have.

Companies come and float their shares on a Stock Exchange to raise capital for expansion. To float on the exchange the company must meet certain requirements of profitability. The capital is raised by selling shares to the public. The share market is made up of large institutions, like fund managers, banks, right down to the ordinary 'mum and dad' investor.

The share market has been around for hundreds of years where traders even traded tulips. Today the financial market is an enormous giant where over $2.5 trillion dollars is transacted in currencies (Foreign Exchange) alone every single day! Investors can trade anything from shares in a company, gold, silver, one currency against another, wheat, corn, even pork bellies and electricity.

The Benefits of Investing in the Share Market are:

- You do not need to rely on suppliers, agents, tradesmen, clients, staff, employers etc. It is simply you and the market.
- You don't need to run any of your decisions past anyone (except your wife, husband, investment partner and/or financial adviser).
- If the UK or USA markets are not open, the Asian or the Australian markets will be.
- You don't need to have an in-depth knowledge of any particular economy, culture or society to trade in that market successfully. You can be living on one side of the world sitting by your pool and trading on the Japanese share market as long as you have an internet or phone connection.

The share market can give you the money,
time and freedom you desire.

You can trade in so many different financial markets and instruments around the world.

The most common markets are the:-

- **Share Market (stocks/shares)**: buying/selling ordinary shares within any company, within any industry, within any country. Stocks are sold by owners of companies to gain additional funding to aid the growth and expansion of their companies. Stocks can either increase or decrease in value resulting in either the earning and sharing of dividend by stockholders when stock prices rise or no dividends being declared to stockholders when there are losses. Shares are purchased by individuals to give them part ownership of a company. Shareholders have a right to vote and are involved in the decision making of the company. Dividends are also declared when there is a profit and none declared when there is a loss.

- **Currency Market (Foreign Exchange, otherwise known as Forex or FX)**: is the trading of one foreign currency for another. The FX is a leveraged trading vehicle where you can gain leverage as high as 200:1. That is powerful, if you had £10,000 in a FX account you could be controlling £2,000,000. The FX also trades 24 hours over 6 days a week so you can join in any time it suits you. This type of investing must be treated with caution as there is great potential for huge losses. Strict risk and money management strategies must be applied and followed.

- **Derivative Market**: (Options, Warrants, Futures and Contracts for Difference) A **derivative gives** one the right to purchase these instruments from the issuer at a specific price; all instruments within this market are also leveraged. It means that they mimic an underlying market, eg; share price, index, currency, equity, commodity or combinations. **Contracts for Difference**—A benefit that Contracts for Difference (CFDs) have over Options and Warrants is that they do not have time limits.

You can continue to hold on to the contract for as long as you like – it will not expire or become worthless. CFDs also have fantastic tools where you can utilise technology. You can place an order to enter the market at a specific level above or below the current market; attach a Stop Loss and walk away and you don't need to watch the screen waiting for the market to reach your desired entry price. (A stop loss is the worst case exit price that you have decided to get out at should the market go against your favour). **Options** have strategies where they act like an Insurance Policy. They can be conservative or speculative; they can be adapted to meet your specific requirements but be aware that they could be very risky for the novice trader and they have a short life span. **Futures** are also known as forward contracts. They bind the seller to provide a commodity or asset to the buyer at a pre-agreed price. **Warrants** are usually issued for a number of years and guaranteed by a company.

Each of these markets and instruments have amazing features that can benefit the investor in their quest for financial freedom, some of these are:-

- **Risk management** tools such as Guaranteed Stop Losses can be used by investors to determine their risk and set a price for a maximum loss for a given trade. The computer system automatically closes down their position and prevents them losing their investment capital other than what they determined and accepted prior to taking on the trade. Investors pay a 'premium' for such a benefit. It is often worth the cost as it saves them 'slipping' in a fast moving market, and it gives them 'peace of mind'.
- **Leverage** allows investors to control parcels of money significantly more than their margin (security deposit). Eg; 10:1 means ten times the amount they have in their trading account. If the investor has £10,000, they have access to trade £100,000. (Interest is paid on the borrowed amount, just like a home loan).
- **With diversification** the share market provides ultimate exposure to various asset classes, sectors, economies, commodities, and currencies.
- **Liquidity** within the financial markets is incredible. Investors can sell down their holding/s and access their cash within a matter of days.
- **Dividends and Capital Growth** are the two forms in which you can make money from the share market. Dividends are equivalent to 'rental income' received from investment properties, whilst capital growth is the increase in the value of the shares (stocks) that you purchased.

- Profit in **rising and declining** markets. We mentioned earlier that informed investors don't sit on their investments and wait for things to work out rather they change their strategy and profit from falling share prices. This strategy is known as **SHORT SELLING or GOING SHORT**. This means that you 'sell before you buy'. Novice investors get confused when they are told that they need to sell their stocks before they buy them, and wonder how they can sell stocks that they don't own yet?

Most Stock Exchanges of the world have lists of companies that you can choose from to 'Short Sell' to. You simply borrow the shares from the Stock Exchange; go to the market and sell your shares hoping that the price falls; then you buy them back again some time in the future at a lower price.

For example: You borrow 1000 shares (from the Stock Exchange) and go to the market and sell them for £10 each. (You now have £10,000 in your pocket, which in reality is the profit/loss set against your trading account). Then in the future if the share price falls down to £6, (in the direction of your favour), you then go back to the market and BUY back 1000 shares-this closes out the position—you then pay £600 to regain ownership of the 1000 shares and this leaves you with £400 in your pocket (trading account).

You will find out that you have profited from the price difference in the transaction, the shares are then returned to the Stock Exchange/ Broker to fulfil your obligations of returning the same number of shares to them.

Short selling through the stock exchange is the 'old and clumsy' way to 'Short Trade' the market. Nowadays it is much easier to go through Contract For Difference (CFD) Providers, Futures or Forex Brokers.

Share Market Analysis Methods:

<u>**Technical**</u> Analysis is a method of evaluating shares by analysing charts which visually display the market activity, past prices, and volume. **Technical Analysts** do not measure a security's intrinsic value; instead they look for patterns and indicators on stock charts that are likely to determine a stock's future direction. Technical Analysts believe that the historical performance of a stock is a strong indication of its future performance and believe that the market's sentiment is reflected in the current price.

<u>**Fundamental**</u> Analysis is another method where **Fundamental Analysts** attempt to measure a company's intrinsic value by comparing related economic and industry conditions, internal financials and management performance with other qualitative and quantitative factors which can affect the share price.

In order to determine which stock to buy or sell, investors often obtain reports produced by these analysts, they read and digest them in order to make an informed decision of when they should enter or exit the market. If there are more buyers than sellers, the market will move upwards; likewise if there are more sellers than buyers, the market will move downwards. This is known as the supply & demand theory. It is very much like how a real estate auction works; the more people that want to buy the one property, the higher the price goes; on the other side, if not many people want to buy the property, the buyer can offer a much lower price.

Only a chart can show us what is actually producing this driving force, through trends, volume and indicators; a chart can also show us where to buy and sell shares, otherwise known as entry and exit points.

This is the key to successful investing whether for short term gain or for long-term growth.

Chart Source: market-analyst.com

Share Broker/Trading Account:

All investors will need to open a Trading Account through;

- a professional Broker Service/Agency, or their Bank for trading in ordinary Shares
- or directly with a Contracts For Difference (CFD) Provider—if they decide to trade in CFD Products
- or a Futures or Foreign Exchange Broker – if they decide to trade in Futures or the Foreign Exchange.

A professional Broker normally charges a higher brokerage fee for additional services such as providing recommendations (advising) on what to buy and sell or where to buy and sell.

_A_ word of caution: Brokers make their money from the brokerage fee (rate) they charge on each and every trade you make, so the more trades you make the more money they make. This at times isn't helpful to your investing as you lose money instead of making a profit.

If you are proficient at selecting your own stock or in understanding a Stock Report or analysts report then it is much more sensible to open a trading account yourself through your own Bank where you can pay a much lower and competitive brokerage fee (rate).

Trading accounts are now often linked with an **online trading platform** where you can easily execute trades yourself online across a wide and varied market. Please note that some of these trading platforms do not accept registrations from residents of some countries. Please check the website of your preferred platform for more details.

Some trading sites to visit are:-

> http://www.forex.com/uk/land-trade-gen.html?src=201304C
>   NS1702&gclid=CP2h4eSdgrcCFSbHtAod-xkAAA
> www.londonstockexchange.com
> www.dogsofthedow.com
> www.bloomberg.com
> http://www.google.com/finance

As an investor the decision as to whether or not to trade in a particular stock and/or market solely rests with you. Obtain relevant information (analysts' and government reports) and digest them or get them explained to you for a fee by a Broker so that when you do invest in the share market you are an informed investor who is aware of all the risks and pitfalls.

You must seek independent financial advice before acting on any of the strategies mentioned in this section. You must not act on the spur of the moment which could cause you financial losses.

Electronic Commerce/Internet Marketing

Electronic Commerce also known as eCommerce or ecommerce involves the process of buying and selling products or services over the internet or other computer network. A product is often transferred from one person to another over the internet.

Internet Marketing is the marketing of products and services over the internet. Individuals and companies market their products by use of affiliates, search engines, display advertisements, emails etc. Individuals and companies using the internet to market themselves often save on costs as they do not need to open a physical office site or employ staff to man their offices.

By marketing on the internet you can reach people globally rather than nationally. You can deal with people of all races, creed and gender; you can also measure the success of your advertising and marketing efforts by making use of any of the statistical analytical tools available in the market.

The shop front has now expanded from the glass panels along the foot path and its immediate community, opening only from 9am-5pm Monday – Friday, to a worldwide audience of 24 hours a day, 7 days a week, as businesses now create their presence online.

The internet has brought businesses to a higher level where competition is now at a global rather than a state or national level. Not only are established businesses marketing online, but also new online businesses that do not have a physical address. This allows the owners the freedom to trade globally without being restricted to any one location.

FACT: There are 2,405,518,376 (billion) internet users in the world as of 30 June 2012, that's a lot of people to sell to. Source: Internet World Stats-

FACT: Over 92% of online consumers have indicated that they are likely to make purchases via the internet in the next year. Good news for all of us. Source: TNS, 2012

FACT: This year, sales via e-commerce will grow 18.3% to $1.298 trillion worldwide, as Asia-Pacific surpasses North America to become the world's No. 1 market for B2C ecommerce sales. Wouldn't you like a small share of this?—Source: eMarketer.com – 2013

FACT: Small businesses that use the Internet have grown 46% faster than those who do not. Source: American City Business Journals

FACT: More than 724,000 people say that eBay is their primary or secondary source of income. Another 1.5 million individuals say they supplement their income by selling on eBay. Source: July 2005 survey conducted for eBay by AC Nielsen International Research

EBay executives told analysts at their eBay's annual investors day on 28th March 2013 that they expect revenue of between $21.5 billion to $23.5 billion in 2015 compared to the $14 billion they generated in 2012 as their company continues to expand globally focusing more on local commerce making use of mobile technology. Source: Reuters.com

FACT: Package Facts says rich consumers are more likely to shop online. Overall, 34 percent of respondents said they made an online purchase over the last year while 50 percent of affluent respondents and 57 percent of the highly affluent used e-commerce. (Wouldn't you rather be selling to people who have money?) Source:, Norman Hallett Marketing

There is no doubt that the World Wide Web is huge and here to stay. In the major developed countries above 63% of the population now have access to the web. Also most of the English-speaking countries and millions of others (300 million) who can speak English are trading on the internet.

Digital products such as software, eBooks, newsletter subscriptions, networking services etc are often sold and bought on the internet. Consumers receive their products instantly (for non-physical digital items) and do not need to wait for delivery by the old snail mail. If a consumer can receive their product from you immediately, at anytime of the day or night, you will most likely be the business that they will buy from.

Be creative and think of an online business which sells both digital products and services. You don't need to be a computer geek to come up with an online business idea, just think about things in your life that have frustrated you . . . the solution could make you very rich as it is likely thousands of others are frustrated just like you.

Services are also sold and bought online (internet) which can be paid for and received immediately. Services such as online businesses (tax returns, company registrations etc); travel online business (recreation, hotels, cars etc); education online services (on-line training, correspondence courses, degrees etc) and family and health online services (psychotherapist, wellbeing information etc).

You can have a website selling information on anything that you have a passion for provided it does not go against common sense, ethics or morals.

There are methods you can apply to market your site, products and services on the first pages of the major search portals so that internet users are directed to your site.

The Different ways of getting to and staying at the top of major search engines

Search engine optimization is the method applied to ensure that your site appears on the top pages of the major/leading search portals thereby ensuring that internet users/portal customers are directed to your site.

You can get your business noticed on the internet in a number of ways, some of which are by:-

1. **Keywords**: This is done by having the right keywords listed on your site so that people can be directed to your site. You must find out what key words your competitors are using to drive traffic to their sites so that you can use them as well. You must make use of the relevancy search engines available so that the keywords you choose are what people are looking for. You must be specific with your key words and not generic. The key words must be relevant to the theme and topic of your site, products and services.

2. **Pay per click search engines (cost per click)**: This is an internet advertising model which you can use to direct traffic to your site. If you can afford to pay to get your site listed on the first pages of search engines then do so. There are many types of search engine advertising networks in the market today that will meet your specific and individual needs or requirements. An example of this is ClickPaid who you can pay a fee to and they will in turn drive traffic to your site. ClickPaid can be found at http://www.clickpaid.com/?r=123492.

3. **Directories: Register your site with directories**. There are free directories that you can register your site on and there are directories that incur a fee for registration. Consider your options thoroughly; registering within trade sites is advantageous because the more credible directories that you

register with, the higher your site gets listed on the search engines.

4. **Use of Meta tags**: This is used to improve your site search relevancy. These are the HTML or XHTML that you will find on sites. By using Meta tags on your site, this places your site higher on the search engines. Relevant keywords are used in the description page, title page and all other relevant pages of your site which draws traffic to your site.

5. **Creating a Profile on Major Social Networking sites**: By having a Profile on the major social networking sites you draw attention and traffic to your site as users will be interested in knowing more about you and what you are offering.

6. **Website Linking:** You can link your site with other sites where you sell related/complimentary products, goods or services. This is a good way of getting to the top of search engines.

7. **Having High Quality and Relevant Material on your site:** People get put off with irrelevant, outdated information and shoddiness on sites. The effect of which leads to negative publicity, bad press, loss of traffic and finally loss of revenue to the site owner. Make sure you keep your site fresh, useful and updated.

EBooks

EBooks are a BRILLIANT digital product that anyone can produce and sell. As people now want to receive their product instantly when they make a purchase they are more likely to buy it from a website which offers them this instant service.

You need to think outside the box when deciding on what product to make for sale. You may own a motorbike and accessories shop in a small isolated town, but this does not stop you from having a shop front on the internet selling the same products to the world. Imagine if you had an EBook called "Your complete guide to DIY motorbike servicing", which people could download at a tiny price of £4.99 or $7.99. This would drive extra traffic to your site and create you another MSI (Multiple Source of Income) which doesn't cost you a penny or cent!

You could even produce a mini-video that people can watch via live streaming which goes with the EBook to show people exactly how to service the bike themselves. There could be a series of EBooks or videos that people could pay a small monthly subscription for. An MP3 can even be inserted into the EBook. You can be as creative as you wish when designing your digital products.

EBooks are a brilliant idea as they don't need to be professionally produced, you can do an amazing job yourself with the software that is already available on your home or work computer.

Clickbank is a fantastic website that allows individuals with digital products to advertise them there for other people to sell, and vice versa, where each party has a share in the sale price, see www. clickbank.com for details.

You can become an affiliate with Clickbank so that you can obtain related digital products/software which will complement your eBooks. These add-ons could be sold by you through your own website, expanding the range of products available for you to sell. You will certainly attract more customers this way and partake in extra revenue.

Building your Business List:

Giving away EBooks is a great way to build your Customer List or Database. People opt-in by providing their name and email addresses through a 'squeeze page', in return for your EBook.

List building can also be done through Giveaway Events. You should type "Giveaway Event" into your internet browser to find businesses that host these events. By providing a digital product you can participate in the event, and build your list very quickly. The events are for a limited time and allow people to give their contact details in return for free digital products.

Virtual Assistant (VA)

Not only are businesses show casing their products and services on line to a worldwide audience, but also individuals are listing their skill sets too in order to take advantage of ongoing projects and jobs.

An entrepreneurial ecommerce idea is www.elance.com. This business brings people together across the world that require projects to be completed by Virtual Assistants in areas such as Finance & Management, Admin Support, Writing & Translation, Design & Multimedia, Sales & Marketing, Engineering, Legal, Proof Reading and Editorial services amongst others.

The benefit is that people can work from home and provide their expertise globally rather than just locally, and they can work whenever it suits them. The projects are listed by the people requiring the services (buyers) and are then bidded upon by the individuals/companies (service providers) that can provide that service, (almost like an EBay for jobs).

The concept of the Elance Business Model is an impressive demonstration of how the virtual assistant model works. There are so many other virtual assistant businesses on the World Wide Web to meet your varying needs and requirements. Check the providers' ratings and score point before you offer your product or services to them.

The investor can also use this model to offer his services in order to create another source of passive income.

As an investor, your talents, skills and abilities are being sought for by others out there who are willing to pay you when you use them for their benefit.

Multi Level Marketing & Affiliate Marketing

Multi Level Marketing and Affiliate Marketing are extremely common and they are embraced ideas in some of the larger developed countries, unfortunately there is quite a lot of suspicion around the concept and it is regularly compared with or called a 'scam' or Ponzi Scheme.

Multi Level Marketing (MLM):This is a business model where people continuously recruit more people below them in a hierarchal fashion, and each new member pays a fee that could be described as a form of 'membership/subscription fee'. Normally a product is sold with this membership fee at the initial sign up stage and then each member is required to pay a regular monthly membership fee. (The product is "there" just for legal reasons as the business needs to be selling something!).

A portion of each membership fee from the people below gets paid to the people above. The more a person recruits people below them, the more money that person gets (have you ever heard of the women empowering women scheme). As people below the first, second and third person continues to recruit more people; those on the first, second and third levels would eventually get a nice passive/residual income stream for themselves.

It is noted that this marketing scheme is lucrative for the people in the upper levels as they would receive a continuous stream of income, sometimes to the detriment of those below them in the chain.

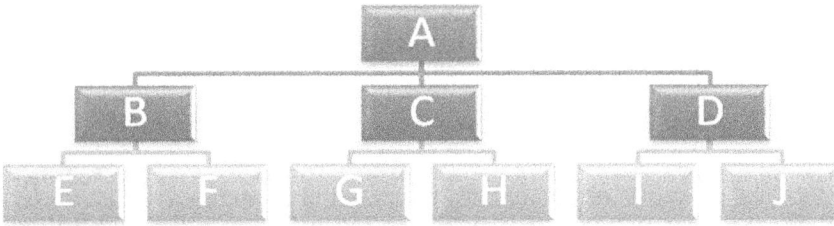

Unfortunately when people are taught 'recruiting' they are often told to focus on the product rather than on the business, an example of which is above. People are told to come to a 'meeting' and are given vague details about the process, when they are at the meeting there is often a lot of hard selling going on and people being pressurised to take advantage of the so called ' limited last minute deals/ opportunity'.

This approach makes people feel obliged to join a MLM which promises loads of money with little or no effort. They are however told that they must recruit other people below them to earn any money, which only works if the people below them also have a good understanding of how powerful this business model works.

If they don't work hard to recruit people themselves then the flow of money to all members on the higher levels will stop. So unless you enjoy networking with other people and informing them of the business opportunities available to them, then Multi Level Marketing is most likely not for you. As you will need to get them excited about the business model, its product and have them see the bigger picture.

If people are well-informed of this business model and are not pressurised into joining this scheme then the MLM systems can be very lucrative.

Affiliate Marketing: is a marketing practice conducted over the internet in which a business (the Grantor) rewards Affiliates

(Grantee) for their marketing efforts in bringing new customers or visitors to their business.

Affiliates refer their customers and/or visitors from their sites to their Grantors site and receive a commission from the Grantor when each customer or visitor purchases an item from the Grantor's site. Sometimes the mere referral of potential customers/visitors to the Grantors' site will result in the Affiliate earning a commission. Affiliates often use emails, display advertising banners and search engine optimisation/marketing tools to advertise their grantors site, products and services and to drive traffic to their grantor's site. Examples of Grantors who pay Affiliates a fee for sending/driving visitors to their Customers' sites is ClickPaid, see: http://www.clickpaid.com/?r=123492 or Profit Wealth Club, see: http://www.profitwealthclub.com/?ref=Destiny.

Most major companies/businesses offer affiliate-ship programmes, notable examples are Amazon.com, Amazon.co.uk and Clickbank. Amazon.com associates place banners or text links on their site for individual books or even provide links directly to Amazon's home page. In order to find out whether a business or company that you are interested in offers an affiliate-ship program, contact the business directly or go to their website as there is often a reference to the affiliate programme on either the top or bottom of their Home Page with a link to direct you to the relevant page.

Please note that before you sign up for any affiliateship programme that you thoroughly read the Grantor's terms and conditions as some conditions are very restrictive and any breach may result in the Grantor suing you. In addition some of the commissions being offered are very negligible.

You may find that in directing customers from your site to your Grantor's site that you may lose your own customers. Never affiliate yourself to products or services that are in direct competition to you or your business as you don't want your customers purchasing your competitors goods and services to your detriment.

Creating Wealth through Business Ownership

A business is carried on to make profit (unless they are a charitable organisation but they will still need to meet their expenses and overheads) and to create wealth for its owners. Businesses provide goods and services to their customers and often sell to the public at large.

You can carry on a business on your own as a sole proprietor/sole trader; with others in the form of a partnership or as a company.

A sole proprietor/sole trader is a business owned by only one person. The sole trader carries on the business on his own or employs others to assist him. He has unlimited personal liability for the debts incurred by the business and he alone enjoys all the profits made. Examples of this type of businesses are vehicle repair garages, a restaurant, and auto washing service, take outs or Beauty Spar services.

A partnership is a form of business where two or more people carry out a business with the sole aim of sharing the losses and enjoying the profit. Each partner is however liable for the total liability of the business incurred by the partnership unless it is a limited partnership. The same examples of businesses mentioned above can be run as a partnership including Accountancy firms, Legal Firms, Medical Consultancies, Recruitment Agencies, however these businesses are much larger.

A company/corporation is a business run for profit and can be limited by shares or by guarantee or an unlimited company/ corporation. The company/corporation has a separate legal personality from its members and it would be liable for its debts (and not its members). The company has an entity of its own; it can be sued for any unpaid debt and enter into contracts in its own name.

The company/corporation is owned by its members and/or its shareholders. A board of directors is employed to oversee the affairs of the business and its employees. The businesses mentioned in both cases above equally apply here. The company enjoys the profit by way of dividends paid to its shareholders and other stake holders.

Although these are the major forms of businesses, they are often run differently depending upon the country of origin and/or local government regulations.

As an investor, you can carry on any of these types of businesses, however you will have to satisfy the legal, taxation and financial regimes applicable before doing so. Some countries require you to be a resident before you can operate a particular form of enterprise. Also depending on what product or service you intend to sell, you would need to fulfil their trade and financial requirements.

Once you have decided that creating wealth through business ownership is a strategy that you want to use, you will then have to consider the following factors which are not exhaustive:-

1. Trading –do you intend to trade as a sole trader, partnership or company/corporation, if as a partnership or corporation, who are your partners, company secretary and directors;
2. Name of your company;
3. Company formation—do you intend to buy a company off the shelf or do you intend to register one brand new;
4. Products and services—what products and/or services do you intend to sell;
5. Market research—is there a demand for your product/s and/or service/s;
6. Who are your competitors;
7. Who are/would be your suppliers and contractors;

8. Location of Company premises—where are you going to trade from –is it the internet or physical location/site;
9. Recruitment of staff , what are your Human Resources' policy on recruitment, promotion, termination and extension of contracts etc;
10. consider health and safety issues and regulation pertaining to your trade;
11. taxation, payroll and returns;
12. VAT—Do you need to register for VAT?
13. IT and internet connections for staff and the business;
14. Taxes—income, corporation and personal taxes;
15. Sales and marketing of company and products/services offered
16. Company lawyer –retaining service of a reputable lawyer;
17. Company account—retaining services of reputable accountant and taxation professionals;
18. How do you protect your business and interests? Would you be obtaining insurance product liability and professional indemnity insurance?

For more detailed information see: Beginners guide to working for yourself/starting up a business at the following web site—www. hmrc.gov.uk/startingup/index.htm.

Chapter 4

Wealth Building Strategies

Portfolio Building

Taking the time to PLAN your portfolio will be one of the most beneficial things you can do as a foundation to your wealth building. There are so many components for you to consider such as:-

BUDGETTING: it is important to get your cash flow in order. You need to ensure there is **more money coming in than going out**. A budget is a brilliant way to ensure that you are keeping your spending under control. If you haven't taken much notice of both your income and expenditure before, following a Budget will be a good strategy for CHANGING YOUR MONEY HABIT.

Obviously you don't want to be too stingy and have a completely boring life by cutting down on all of life's luxuries. It is important therefore that you look at other income avenues and continuously work on adding new MSI's (Multiple Sources of Income) that will eventually replace your current income.

95

DEBT REDUCTION: There are two types of debt – Good Debt & Bad Debt.

- Bad debt are all those credit cards and loans which you have accumulated over the years for items which depreciate in value, eg; TV, white goods, clothing etc which you are still paying for many times over because of a high interest rate. Most of these goods are no longer "current" and need upgrading.
- Good Debt is when you borrow money, invest it and receive a return higher than the interest you are paying. For example, investment loan where you borrowed the money for 8% per annum and your investment returns you over 15% per annum (net return = 7%).

BREAKING BAD HABITS: You will need to break out of bad habits of investing in downward investments, procrastination (putting off making decisions making until the last minute) having a negative self image, bad attitude and choices.

BREAKING BAD HABITS AND REPLACING THEM WITH GOOD ONES: In order for you to achieve your dreams of financial freedom you will have to replace bad habits for good ones. This would require great effort, time and dedication on your part. Good habits such as investing in upwards investments, having a positive self image, having the right attitude and making the right choices is what you will have to adopt.

REPITITION: In order for the good habits to embed, you would need to keep repeating them until they become part and parcel of you. You will need to achieve a level of unconscious competence so that you can respond automatically without having to think consciously of it.

FOCUSSING ON THE RESULTS: you will need to focus on the results you desire i.e. financial freedom by keeping your goals always before you as this would keep you on track in challenging times and moments of discouragement.

INVESTMENTS: Here you need to decide what investment strategy or style best suites you. Do you prefer Real Estate, Shares, businesses etc? What suits your personality the most and what fits best in with your lifestyle goals? When adversity strikes, it would be much easier for you to remain persistent in the face of it because the strategy chosen is something you love. What are you most passionate about? How much investment capital will you start off with?

SAVINGS: Set up an automatic debiting facility from your bank account in which income is paid into, and have a minimum of 10% go directly into a savings account with good returns. This should happen regularly (weekly OR monthly) for ALL INCOME that you generate. Once this builds up you can transfer it to another higher yielding vehicle within your Portfolio.

MULTIPLE SOURCES OF INCOME: Focus on regularly adding MSI's over time. Don't take on too many things at once as this can be ineffective and lead to you being exhausted. Get one started, and as the flow of income starts coming in turn your attention to another.

INSURANCE: It is very important to factor in some insurance protection so that your portfolio does not crumble when your major source of income suddenly stops in the event of sickness, accident, or redundancy. When you are building a portfolio and acquiring investments it is very important that you do not over expose yourself, especially when leveraging. It is crucial to build in **'buffers'** so that in emergencies your investments becomes **SELF FUNDING.**

A strategy for self funding within a share portfolio may be, if you have £50,000 of your own money with the leverage potential to control £500,000 (10% margin), you would not over expose yourself by using the full £50,000.

Instead you would only use £25,000 (leveraged to £250,000) and the balance of your capital, (£25,000) is kept as a buffer for interest repayments should your income stop. This means your portfolio is self funding and would not become affected for quite some time.

The Power of Leveraging

This is a strategy that will catapult you to financial freedom. The wealthy use this powerful concept to get ahead quicker.

Leverage is simply borrowing more money for more buying power for investments i.e. Other People's Money (OPM). Just like when you purchased your own home or an investment property with a loan even though you only had the deposit amount available.

For example you can purchase a property valued at £250,000 with a £25,000 deposit. If the property has capital growth of 10% (£25,000) you have just made a 100% return on your investment, (not considering costs).

Leverage can also be used in other investment vehicles such as businesses and the share market. **However** just as there is the potential of significant profit so also there is the potential to make huge losses, therefore it is essential that you understand and implement **strict money & risk management principles.**

People with a poverty mindset are afraid of leveraging because of the large number of disaster stories they hear and read about. These disasters occur because many people try to 'get rich overnight' and don't apply sound judgment when making decisions.

Chapter 5

Tax and Tax Planning

Tax is a very complex area and one that is ever changing, though it tends to be the details that change rather than the basic structure of the tax regime which tends to stay very much the same.

Because of this complexity and the ever changing rules and regulations, it is strongly recommended that you seek the advice of a specialist tax advisor or accountant, both of whom have a remit to minimise your tax bill, if your income (and tax bill) is high or your affairs are complex.

Notwithstanding this, there are things you can do to reduce your tax bill, the first step of which is to get a basic understanding of the tax system in the country in which you are resident and/or your business is situated.

Taxes that you may be liable for

There are certain taxes which we all pay every day and which we can only avoid by changing our behaviour – taxes on fuel (petrol and diesel), on transport (road fund licence) and on alcohol. Our only choice is to switch to something that attracts less tax (public transport) and to drink less or abstain completely.

Other taxes are different. Here we can adopt strategies to minimise the amount of tax we pay. These taxes include the following:

**Income Tax
(IT)**

Income tax is the biggest source of revenue for the government. It is the tax that individuals pay on their income, either through the PAYE system if they are employed or via the self-assessment system if they are self-employed. It is a banded, progressive system, with a personal allowance and then bands of higher taxation up to the highest rate (45% from 2013).

Because this is such an important tax it is the one which tends to be where the greatest potential savings are and where your strategy should concentrate.

In the UK, the tax rates and allowances change from year to year, usually in the Budget (late March) and sometimes in the Autumn Statement (November or December). For the periods 2014-15, the personal allowance for those born after 5 April 1948 will be increased to £10,000, and the basic rate limit will be reduced to £31,865. For current tax rates and allowances you should consult the HMRC website (www.hmrc.gov.uk) and follow the links to the appropriate tax. In the case of Income Tax this is http://www.hmrc.gov.uk/rates/it.htm.

**National
Insurance (NI)**

Although often neglected, National Insurance Contributions are a tax. They are included automatically in PAYE but are separately calculated for self-employed people. For the latter, tax payers are recommended to check whether they are paying NIC's at the correct rate (see http://www.hmrc.gov.uk/rates/nic.htm)

**Corporation
Tax**

Corporation tax is the equivalent tax to income tax for companies. There are two basic rates, one for small companies with profits not exceeding £300,000 (in 2013 this was at 20%) and one for large companies (23% in 2013 falling to 21% in 2014). It should be noted that the rate for both is well below the higher tax rate for income tax. For high earners, it might be wise to consider switching to a company structure for their taxation.

Again this is a tax whose rates change from year to year; particularly when the Government is trying to encourage economic growth (they lower the rates to encourage enterprise). To check the current rates refer to the HMRC website (http://www.hmrc.gov.uk/rates/corp.htm)

Value Added Tax (VAT)

Value Added Tax is a consumption tax and, as the name suggests, is a tax on value ADDED to a product and/or service as it proceeds from business to business and finally onto the end user or consumer. To give a simple example of how this works, if you consider a nail this will have gone from mine where the ore is extracted, to a smelting works where the metal is refined, to the nail maker and finally to the retailer who sells it onto a customer, a householder. VAT will be added at each stage but each business can recover the VAT they incur because they are not the end user. It is the retailer who is the final collector of the VAT from the householder, and it is this proportion (less the input VAT) that is sent to HMRC. Only the end user, the householder, effectively pays the VAT.

There are three rates of VAT, depending on the goods or services the business provides. The rates are:

standard—20 per cent
reduced—5 per cent
zero—0 per cent

There are also some goods and services that are exempt from VAT or outside the UK VAT system altogether.

It is clear that, if you are a business, there are distinct advantages in being registered for VAT because you can reclaim your input VAT, however preparing VAT returns takes time and has to be done accurately so many businesses below the automatic threshold for VAT (In 2013 this is a £77,000 pa turnover) choose not to elect. For current rates of VAT and rules refer to the HMRC website (http://www.hmrc.gov.uk/vat/forms-rates/rates/index.htm)

Capital Gains Tax (CGT)

Capital Gains Tax is a tax on the realised appreciation in value of an asset. This is important; the tax is only on the change in value and it is only payable when the asset is disposed of—usually therefore when it is sold.

The significance of this will be discussed below but it should be noted that the tax rates on Capital Gains is considerably lower than that on Income (at least at the higher rate) and there are considerable allowances to individuals for capital gains every year.

The following Capital Gains Tax rates currently apply:

18 per cent and 28 per cent tax rates for individuals (the tax rate you use depends on the total amount of your taxable income, so you need to work this out first) 28 per cent for trustees or for personal representatives of someone who has died 10 per cent for gains qualifying for Entrepreneurs' Relief

As with all taxes, you should check the current rates and allowances via the HMRC website (http://www.hmrc.gov.uk/rates/cgt.htm)

Inheritance Tax

Inheritance tax is the tax which is paid on the transfer of assets, usually on death. Chapter 6 deals with this Tax in more detail. You should be aware that the threshold is high before inheritance tax falls due (currently £325,000). The tax is at 40% on the value of assets above this amount. As with all taxes, you should check the current rates and allowances via the HMRC website:

http://www.hmrc.gov.uk/rates/iht-thresholds.htm.

Council Tax or Uniform Business Rate (UBR)

These taxes are on occupation of property, the former for residential property, and the latter on commercial premises (shops, offices, industrial buildings etc.). The former, a simple band based system can be appealed only in very limited circumstances and must be made within specified time frames. There are some reliefs available – if you are unemployed or if you are in single occupation, for example. The latter (commercial) assessment is more complex and might be worth appealing if you occupy such premises – though there are rules dealing with when an appeal can be made (see the Valuation Office Agency website for more details about these subjects: http://www.voa.gov.uk/corporate/index.html) .

Stamp Duty   Stamp duty and Stamp Duty Land Tax. These are a tax on specific transactions including share transactions (stamp duty) and on the sale and leasing of property (SDLT).

There are different rates on non-residential and mixed-use properties. As with all tax rates, you should check at the HMRC website for the rates applicable (http://www.hmrc.gov.uk/sdlt/intro/rates-thresholds.htm).

The tax system is complex and is made more so by rules relating to what is and is not taxable and also because of tax reliefs. Reliefs are measures the government puts in place to either help certain parts of the community who may be struggling financially or are disadvantaged, such as the elderly or those on low incomes. It is also introduced to encourage taxpayers to take actions which are beneficial to the country. These include saving for the future, paying towards a pension fund or investing in new businesses which if successful will boost employment and the economy.

Tax planning is about being wise about how you structure your finances by utilising tax reliefs available to you. We will cover the latter briefly at the end of this chapter.

You should also be aware of the tax implications of all that you do and incorporate this into your decision making processes. Your house, as your principle private residence, is exempt from Capital Gains Tax (this is one of the reasons for the boom in property values as investing in your own property is very tax efficient) however second homes and buy-to-let properties are subject to CGT.

Similarly if you sell shares and Gilts (Government backed loan stock), or gold or works of art, you may be liable for CGT. Income from shares (dividends), interest from Gilts and rent from property all count as income and will be taxed as such. Investment decisions need to be made taking all these into account as they incur CGT.

Ten Strategies that can help reduce your tax bill

1. The first strategy is simple: If you are paying a lot of tax, hire a tax consultant or accountant. This is almost guaranteed to save at least their fee in the tax savings and probably an awful lot more.
2. Do not be tempted to evade tax, hide income or operate as part of the 'black economy'. This will almost certainly cost you much more in the long term as the HMRC are very good at tracking down evaders and the penalties are severe.
3. Turning to more positive strategies for saving tax, one of the simplest is exploring ways of making more of your income come from tax free sources –
    -   Some investment income is tax free. This includes NS&I certificate interest, Interest from ISA's and Child Trust Funds, interest on certain Friendly Society accounts and dividends on ordinary shares in venture capital trusts.
    -   Up to £4250 of income from letting out a room in your house is tax free under the rent a room scheme (note the room has to be furnished).
    -   If you are employed note that some work related expenses reimbursed by your employer (and with prior agreement with HMRC) are tax free. Also if you use your car for work (but not for just travelling to work) then, subject to mileage limits, you can claim relief for the costs.
    -   Maintenance from a former spouse are tax free as is income from life assurance policies and mortgage insurance income for policies taken out against job loss or illness.
    -   And, for the optimistic, premium bond winnings and other gambling earnings is tax free!—in the UK at least.
4. If you are a couple then you should look to distribute income to your greatest advantage. The days of married couple's allowances are gone (unless you were born before

1935) and therefore everyone is treated as an individual for tax purposes. You can, however, move income about, particularly if one of the couple is a higher rate tax payer and the other is a non-taxpayer or pays tax at the basic rate. Considerable savings can be made in this way.

5. If you are employed, check that your PAYE code is correct. According to the National Audit Office, around 30% of PAYE codings are incorrect. You may be paying too much tax but even if you are paying too little it is worth correcting it as underpaid tax often has to be repaid in one lump sum.

6. If you are self-employed then you will have to use the HMRC's self-assessment service. This can be done either using a paper version (deadline 30th October after the tax year has finished in April) or the on-line service (deadline 31st January). To ensure that you minimise the cost to yourself:

    a. Make certain that you meet these deadlines. There is a £100 fine for submitting late and you can be charged interest on the late payment of the tax you owe;

    b. Keep good records that are well structured. This will enable you to submit an accurate return on time as well as ensuring that you count all possible deductions against income, thus reducing your tax bill.

    c. Get to know what the allowable expenses against your income are. If you are doing the tax return yourself, you should spend some time on the HMRC website (www. hmrc.gov.uk) where the rules are laid out reasonably clearly.

    d. Note that if you are also employed and subject to PAYE you can elect to spread your tax payments out over the next tax year by making an adjustment to your PAYE code.

7. Ensure that you claim all the Tax Credits that you are due. The Tax Credits system is a misnomer; Tax Credits are, in fact, a benefit but they are effectively tax-free income.

They are also not automatically given or calculated, you have to apply for them each year. There are two types of Tax Credit; Child Tax Credit and Working Tax Credit. Child Tax Credit is paid when you have a dependent child under 16 (or between 16-19 if in certain types of education and training) and if your income is below certain levels (2012-13, £26,000 if you have one child, up to £32,200 if you have 2 children etc.). Working Tax Credit is there to help people with low incomes even though they work (it also applies to the self-employed, so might help in the early stages of setting up a new business). The claimant has to be over 25 and work over 30 hours per week and be earning less than £13,253 if you're single and childless or £18,023 jointly if you are part of a couple in the 2012-13 tax year.

8. If you are running a business from home you may be able to set off some of your mortgage interest payments against your business profits.

9. If you are liable for substantial amounts of income tax, consider switching your investment from income producing ones to ones that mainly appreciate in capital value. There are a number of reasons why this is tax-efficient under the current rules;

    a. In addition to the reliefs individuals get for income tax, each individual is currently allowed an annual Capital Gains allowance of £10,600 per year. This is the gains in value that can be realised in each tax year before tax is due.

    b. CGT is not paid on the total value of the asset but on that assets increase in value from the time that you bought it

    c. CGT is only paid on realised gains – you only get charged on the gain when you sell or dispose of it (and note that gifts between spouses are tax exempt)

    d. The tax rate on capital gains is generally lower than on income: For 2013-2014 the following Capital Gains Tax rates apply:

- 18 per cent and 28 per cent for individuals (the tax rate you use depends on the total amount of your taxable income and gains)
- 28 per cent for trustees or personal representatives
- 10 per cent for gains qualifying for Entrepreneurs' Relief (source:HMRC)

10. Fundamentally, you can save considerable tax by getting to know the tax relief system. As stated above, the tax relief system is used by the Government to help taxpayers and encourage certain activities. One of the biggest is investment in a personal pension; the tax relief given makes it worthwhile even for non-taxpayers to pay into a personal pension. The gift-aid system encourages gifts to charitable organisations but is very good at offsetting profits and income to the individual. Certain investments are encouraged for those willing to take on risks and put money into new companies through the Enterprise Investment Scheme and the Venture Capital Trusts system, both of which give 30% relief on moneys invested. The other big tax relief are ISA's, individual savings accounts, designed by the Government to encourage savings. Incomes from ISA's are tax free and tax payers should seek to use their ISA allowance each year as this will cumulatively build up to give a substantial tax free income.

The tax system in general and tax reliefs in particular do change in detail every year. Understanding the system and what you can claim and get relief on is an important part of managing your wealth.

For developments in this area and for the tax rates and rules at the time of reading, you are encouraged to consult the HMRC website at: http://www.hmrc.gov.uk/ or your own Government's equivalent website.

Chapter 6

Inheritance Tax

It is an old adage that there are two certainties in life; death and taxes. It should be no surprise therefore that with death *come* taxes – in the UK this is a system called Inheritance Tax (IT).

Although many people do not like to think about their own mortality, it is important not to ignore it in financial planning, particularly if you want to ensure that your wealth is passed on to your spouse/partner, children and/or grandchildren and not have substantial amounts of it taken by the state in tax.

There are actions that you can take to minimise the amount taken in tax and maximise the wealth that that you can pass on to your family. It takes careful planning and this is why we have created a specific chapter here for this subject.

The rules regarding IT are relatively simple but the nuances can be complex. You need to have a good understanding of them before you can put your plan into place.

Inheritance Tax: The basics

Inheritance Tax is due on a person's estate (their property and possessions) when its value exceeds certain limits on death. In the 2013-14 Tax Year this is £325,000. Tax is due at 40% on values above this amount though this may be reduced to 36% if more than 10% of the estate is left to charity.

Note that this is an INDIVIDUAL allowance. Since October 2007, married couples and civil partners can effectively increase these thresholds to £650,000 by transferring the 'nil band' (i.e. the £325,000 allowance) from the first spouse/civil partner to the second. This is not an automatic transfer; it has to be applied for, but can be done at any time after death. Only the unused proportion of the 'nil band' can be passed. It should also be noted that all assets can be transferred between spouses and civil partners tax free prior to death, as long as the person receiving the assets lives in the UK.

These above mentioned limits are generous as a result majority of the UK population fall below the Inheritance Tax threshold.

Under current government plans, the tax-free nil-rate band for IHT will be frozen until 2017/18. This supersedes their announcement in the Autumn Statement of 2012 that increased the level to £329,000 in 2015/16. In addition the Chancellor announced plans to further stamp down on IHT avoidance schemes. HMRC will change the existing treatment of liabilities, setting new rules on when deductions would be allowable or restricting the deduction altogether so as to avoid any possible tax advantage. This measure is in support of the government's anti-avoidance strategy. For developments in this area and for the tax rates and rules at the time of reading, you are encouraged to consult the HMRC website at: http://www.hmrc.gov.uk/rates/inheritance.htm or your own Government's equivalent website.

IT is normally paid by the executors of the will rather than the recipients of the bequest, though there are some rare circumstances when the recipients can be liable. If the estate is held in Trust then it is usually the Trustees who are responsible. IT is normally paid no more than 6 months after the death of the person.

Obviously, on death, the estate must be assessed to see whether it is above or below the IT threshold. This may entail some expense as some valuations may require the employment of specialist professionals to determine an accurate valuation. Land and Property may require the services of a RICS qualified valuer (not an estate agent – the 'valuations' produced by agents have no legal standing).

Similarly if fine arts and chattels are involved a specialist qualified valuer may be required. Some assets are easier to value independently; stocks and shares can easily be valued by reference to stock market listings whilst Government stocks and bonds can be valued for free using Computershare on application to the UK's Office for Debt Management (although they will need to see a Death Certificate beforehand), though if the holdings are extensive and complex, a valuation by a stockbroker may be advisable. Other assets that have to be included are business partnerships and businesses owned wholly or partly by the deceased.

Note that the key value of all assets is the net value. Any debts or liabilities to a business or against other assets (for example outstanding mortgage balances on investment properties) should be deducted to determine the real value.

Tax Planning for Inheritance

There are plans that can be put in place that can greatly reduce the tax liability however these are not short term ones; IT planning should be done as early as possible.

The basic strategy involved with IT planning is the use of the gift system. At this stage it is worth flagging up that the rules are slightly different for your home and other assets, and that the rules vary for gifts between spouses and civil partners and other family members, including children. These are outlined below.

Firstly, we will introduce an important concept, the Potentially Exempt Transaction (PET). A PET is essentially a gift. It is only potentially exempt because it has to be made 7 years before death to be totally exempt; if death occurs within the 7 year period before death then some relief is available – this is called 'Taper Relief'.

Years after Gift when death of donor occurs	Taper Relief Given
1—3 years	Nil
3-4 years	20%
5-6 years	60%
6-7 years	80%

It should be noted, however, that except for the home of the donor, the value gifts (cash and assets) are limited in total to the nil band limit (i.e. currently £325,000). Any gifts in excess of this amount made to people other than the donors spouse or civil partners, will be liable to IT. To explain this, if a donor gifts £100,000 per year to their children, this will be tax free until year 4 when the £325,000 threshold is reached. The £75,000 excess will be taxed at 40%.

There are other exempt donees. These include:

- A qualifying charity based in the EU or other countries;
- National institutions such as museums, universities and the National Trust;
- Any UK political party which has at least 2 seats in the House of Commons (or 1 seat and a national vote exceeding 150,000

There are other exempt gifts that you should be aware of, although they do not strictly form part of your long term Inheritance Tax planning –

- There is an annual exemption of one-off gifts up to £3000 in any tax year (and can be rolled over to a maximum of one year)
- Gifts by a parent for a wedding or civil partnership ceremony up to £5000 (£2500 for gifts from grandparents and anyone else £1000)
- Individuals can give any number of gifts up to a value of £250 to as many different individuals as they like.

Let us now turn specifically to what is often the most important and most valuable single asset in an inheritance, the donor's home.

Firstly it should be remembered that transfer of assets from spouse to spouse (and between civil partners) is exempt. However, you can also gift your house to your children or anyone else and, no matter what it is worth, will continue to be exempt as long as you continue to live for 7 years after the gift is made.

This gift has to be done carefully. If there are any conditions that are applied to it then the tax authorities can determine it to be a 'gift with reservations' – in this case the asset will not be exempt from IT.

What can and can't you do as regards your home?

You CAN'T –
- Give your home away then continue to live in it rent free
- Give your home away and live in it at a nominal or low rent
- Sell your home, give the proceeds to your children and move into a 'granny flat' in their home

You CAN –
- Make short visits and stay for short stays at a home you have given to your children or another person

- Continue to live in the home you have given away as long as you pay the market rent
- Sell your home and give the cash to your children as long as you do not benefit from the cash and do not die within 7 years of the gift.

This latter point can be made more complex if your children and yourself sell your homes and combine the proceeds to buy a bigger house for you all to live in. In this case an apportionment would have to be made; the part paid for by the gift would not be tax exempt.

Summary

We would all like to pass on our wealth to our children and grandchildren. Inheritance Tax is a potential problem in that it can substantially affect what we can pass on. It cannot be completely avoided, but with good planning, its impact can be greatly reduced.

The final proviso, as in both tax sections, is that, although there is a lot you can do yourself, for absolute security and peace of mind you should seek Legal advice from a Solicitor specialising in Inheritance Tax Law, advice from an Independent Financial Advisor and/or Tax Consultant.

Chapter 7

Dealing with debt

Getting into debt is something that can happen to anyone at any time. In today's world, credit and borrowing is relatively easy – mortgages, credit cards, car loans, personal loans and HP agreements – your borrowing can easily add up. Add to that are the goods that make modern life easier and more pleasant – mobile phones, pay TV and the like. It is easy to lose track of how much debt and outgoings have mounted up but, for many, things are fine whilst times are good.

But what happens when things go wrong?

You may be taken ill and be unable to work, or a partner or child is sick that you have to look after. You may lose your job or be made redundant. A business venture may fail or a crucial customer goes bankrupt owing you money. Interest rates may rise sharply or fuel costs increase – in fact a hundred things can happen, particularly when economic conditions are difficult but the results are usually the same – you find it difficult (if not impossible) to meet your outgoings and your debts rise.

It can all seem very bleak in these times. It is easy to get into a mind-set where you try to ignore your problems, sweep them under the carpet, hoping that they will go away or that something will turn up. Doing nothing will just make the situation to get worse as ignoring your creditors will just antagonise them. Speaking to your creditors early and openly is always the best option.

You can get free advice from the Government—see (www.gov.
uk/options-for-paying-off-your-debts/overview) or the voluntary
sector such as the National Debt Line (www.nationaldebtline.
co.uk) or the Citizens Advice Bureau (http://www.adviceguide.org.
uk).

Beware though. There are a lot of 'for profit' companies who will
offer to solve your debt problems. These companies often sound
very convincing, offering very tempting sounding solutions
and an easy way out of your problems. It is rarely that easy and,
all-too-often, these companies offer little more than you can get
for free elsewhere – and remember that these companies are not
charities; they are in business to make money, and that money will
come from you.

The other thing to strongly avoid is turning to short-term lenders,
either the legal ones who advertise on TV or the illegal, unregulated
Loan Shark. The short-term lenders are able to afford TV advertising
because they make huge profits out of their lending – the interest
rates they charge are often as high as 1000%, sometimes over
4000% p.a. They look to be a good stop gap to ease you over an
immediate crisis but continual borrowing at these rates will bleed
you dry.

So, what can you do to tackle your debt problem?

There are four main steps to a good debt management plan.

1. Make sure you are getting all of the income you are entitled
   to
2. Work out your personal/household budget
3. Prioritise the debts
4. Use an appropriate solution to address your debt problem.

Let us look at each in turn.

1. Make sure you are getting all of the income you are entitled to

Many people get into debt because their income does not match their expenditure, however it is also true that many people do not act to maximise their income. One immediate help when debt is mounting is to ensure that everything that can come into the household actually is:

- Benefits and Tax Credits – Many people, particularly those who have worked or run businesses all of their lives have no idea of the benefits that they are entitled to when times get hard. Today, even people in work and the self-employed are entitled to support; those with children are entitled to Child Tax Credit (a benefit which has to be applied for, it is not automatic). There is assistance for paying rent AND help with mortgage interest payments. The system is not for scroungers, it was designed originally partially as a safety net for people who fell on hard times. The system is there, do not hesitate to use it.
- Similarly, are you entitled to a hardship grant from the Social Fund?
- Are you paying too much tax? – Seek advice from either an advisor or free advice from your local Tax Office.
- Can you gain extra income in some way? – A good way may be to rent out a spare room in your home (remember some of this is tax free) or to sell surplus assets via either an electronic auction house like Ebay or by taking a place in a car boot sale.
- Is everyone in your household paying their way? Is there a grown-up child or another working adult in the household who could contribute more?

Some of these steps may seem a little drastic, however having extra cash coming into a household can greatly ease the debt problem.

2. Work out your personal/household budget

It may seem strange putting this second but to do this process accurately you need to know what income you have before you can do these calculations.

There are illustrations and blank forms for working out a budget at the national debt line's web site which can be obtained at www.nationaldebtline.co.uk.

The top part of the budget deals with income. Put down everything coming into the household:

- Wages and salaries
- Benefits and Tax Credits
- Contributions from other people living in your home
- Income from investments
- Income from things like insurance policies and pensions
- Other Streams of Income

The next step is to calculate outgoings:

- Essential spending
    - o Regular payments – rent/mortgage payments, pension contributions
    - o Council Tax
    - o Water Rates
    - o Gas and Electric
    - o TV Licence
    - o Magistrate Court Fines
    - o Maintenance/Child Support
    - o Hire Purchase Goods and Cars
    - o Childcare Costs
    - o Adult Care Costs
    - o Etc.
- Phone costs

- Travel costs
  - o Essential (e.g. travel to work)
  - o Non-essential
- Housekeeping costs – cleaning, clothing, shoes etc.
- Other spending
  - o Hobbies
  - o Leisure
  - o Gifts
  - o TV subscriptions
  - o Smoking
  - o Drinking
  - o Prescriptions (can be free if claiming some benefits)
  - o School Dinners (note that there is a cheaper alternative; sandwiches, hence this is not an essential expenditure)
  - o Etc.

If this is done accurately then you will have a much better understanding of where you stand and whether there is still a shortfall. It can suggest ways forward, for example, is there anything non-essential which you can cut back on? This might also be the point where you can identify things to sell on Ebay or in a car boot sale.

If things are still bad and there are bills that you cannot pay or debts that have mounted up, it is essential to go onto the next step and prioritise your debts.

3. Prioritise the debts

This is very important as certain creditors have the right to:

- Take away your home (repossession/eviction)
- Cut off your gas or electricity (disconnection)
- Send in a bailiff to take belongings from your home to sell (distraint)
- Ask a magistrate to send you to prison

Some creditors can even take action without first going to court first (HMRC can send in bailiffs whilst Gas and Electricity companies can disconnect you without a court order).

Let us look at the high priority debts.

Mortgage lenders

It is absolutely important that priority is given to keeping your home. If you have mortgage arrears or have realised that paying your mortgage is going to be difficult, then you should do the following:

- Contact them early, by phone, in writing or make an appointment to go to see them. Explain exactly what your position is. Show them your household budget.
- Check whether you have mortgage protection insurance and have grounds for a claim
- Offer to pay as much as you can
- If you are in receipt of benefits, the Department of Work and Pensions (DWP) will pay at least some of the interest on your home mortgage (not, of course, on a buy-to-let mortgage) under the Support for Mortgage Interest (SMI) scheme.
- In the longer term there are bigger steps you can take. One is to downsize, selling a large property to buy a more affordable one Another is to approach a Housing Association, who may be willing to buy your home off you and rent it back to you so you become a tenant.

It is very important to pay your mortgage first before any of your unsecured debts (i.e. ones that are not tied to your house such as credit card arrears). Ultimately, your lender has the right to repossess your house if you fail to pay the debt, and to sell off the property to recover the debt. If you are in negative equity (the value of your house being less than the value of the loan), then your mortgage lender has the right to pursue you for the shortfall.

Addressing the issue as early as possible will maximise your chances of avoiding this.

Rent Arrears

If you are a tenant, your rent has to be one of your highest priority debts as you can be evicted if you fail to pay your rent and get in arrears. If paying your rent becomes a problem then you should do the following:

- Contact your landlord early to explain your problem. If you have arrears, offer to pay it off over a longer period of time
- Always pay as much as you can, even if this means not paying other debts
- Check whether you are entitled to housing benefit or Local Housing Allowance
- Check whether the arrears have been calculated correctly
- Get some free advice from sources such as the CAB and Shelter – who are experts in housing matters

You should note that some of the most common types of residential occupational agreement, the Assured Short-hold, offers the tenant very little security. Notwithstanding this, your landlord will need to take you to court to evict you. Landlords are not normally able to use bailiffs to seize your goods to pay off arrears.

Council Tax

Your council tax should be classified as a priority debt. The council tax is the principle source of income for local authorities, so they take non-payment very seriously. The council can resort to distraint and send in the bailiffs to seize assets and, ultimately, can ask the magistrates to send you to prison for non-payment.

Your steps in dealing with Council Tax are similar to dealing with the other priority bills:

- Contact the council as soon as possible to explain what the situation is
- Prioritise payments to this and keep paying as much as you can afford
- Some councils will let you switch from monthly to weekly payments which are often easier to budget for
- Don't forget you can get a 25% reduction for single adult occupancy of a dwelling and there are also reliefs if there is anyone living with you who is mentally or physically disabled
- You also may be able to get Council Tax Benefit and certain other benefits (Income Support, Pension Credit, Job Seeker's Allowance, etc.) or if you are on a low income (currently less than £16,000 p.a.)

Gas and Electricity

Gas and Electricity companies can cut off your supply if you do not pay them, although this should only be done as a last resort. They should offer you a range of payment options first.

If you are in arrears with your gas and electricity payments:

- Contact them early to discuss the problems you are having. The companies are very sensitive to bad publicity at a time when energy bills are rising sharply so they tend to be receptive and helpful to early consultations
- Check that the bill is based on accurate readings and not on estimates. This can lead to the companies temporarily overcharging you
- If the bill is accurate, the options the company can offer you include time to pay back arrears, budget plans where you pay the same amount each period (normally fortnightly)

and also pre-payment meters where you pay in advance for your gas and electricity (note, although this stops arrears accumulating, you cannot be forced to accept a pre-payment meter)

Other priority bills that you should look to pay before any others are:

- Magistrate's Court Fines
- Parking Penalty Fines
- Child Maintenance and Child Support

Failure to pay all of these can lead to further, potentially criminal, action.

The next type of bills in order of importance are ones that, in certain circumstances, become priority ones.

These include benefit overpayments. These can arise either from claiming benefits that you are not entitled to or, and this is quite common, overpayments for Working Tax Credit and Child Tax Credit (this is because both are based on a forecast of the next year's income—if you earn more, then you can find you have been paid too much).

The DWP will, however, come to an arrangement with you if there is an overpayment and there is genuine hardship to you in making a repayment or if you are now on other benefits. They can also write off these debts, the best solution is to talk early to them.

Tax debts tend to have to be prioritised over all others as Income Tax, National insurance and VAT are collected by HMRC who have immense powers to collect what is owed to them. Again, it is very important to talk to them openly as early as you can.

The final sets of important debts are those made under HP or Credit Agreements. If you fail to make payments on these, the creditor can ask to have the goods returned and they can sell them to repay the debt. If you have paid less than $1/_3$ of the amount due, they may be able to repossess the goods without a court order. The failure to pay will also impact on your credit status (see later).

Note that you cannot sell goods bought under these contracts without the permission of the creditor, even if you are using the funds to pay off the debt. This is because you do not own the goods until the final payment is made. (This is also why you should check when buying something like a car second hand that there is no finance owing on it. If there is, then the vendor does not have the right to sell and, if you buy, you do not get title to the goods and you could find yourself out of pocket.)

As to how you should treat these debts depends on a number of things. If it is something like a car or van which you need for your work or travelling to work, then this must become a priority bill and you should pay as much as you can and come to an arrangement with the creditor. If not, then it should have a lower priority, however your credit status will be damaged and you may be losing the ability to get credit in the future.

<u>Dealing with other, low-priority, debts</u>

The strategy with dealing with your other debts (credit, store cards, mobile phone bills, etc.) are as follows:

- Do not ignore them completely. They can still damage your credit record
- Contact your creditors early. Explain that you are struggling. This should buy you more time
- Deal with the most pressing ones first, e.g. the ones where legal action has started against you.

- Open a 'safe' bank account. All banks are required to offer basic bank accounts that do not allow overdrafts but do allow standing orders and direct debits. This account should be in an institution which you do not owe money to and so is safe from being raided to pay other debts. This will give you a way of making payments to your creditors without interference – as long as there is money in it of course.

4. Use an appropriate solution to address your debt problem.

To a certain extent we have already covered some of the strategies that you should employ to deal with at least the early stages of a debt problem. You will have spotted the common themes of contacting your creditors, being open with them and trying to come to an arrangement to at least buy you time and space.

This is always the best option if you can do it. Hopefully, this may give you the opportunity to solve your problems and get your debt under control. This next section will, therefore, concentrate on what you can do if this does not work. Basically these are the things you should resort to if things are more serious.

Debt Consolidation

Many companies offer this and, superficially, it looks to be an attractive option. Essentially, what these companies do is to take over your individual debts, paying off your creditors. You now only have a single creditor – the company – and, usually, pay a lower overall payment to them than you would to your original creditors. This reduces your monthly costs and makes the management of the debt easier as you are now only dealing with a single creditor. However, these companies often require you to secure the new loan against the security of your home so unsecured debt (one that would not see your home repossessed) becomes one with much greater potential consequences. You should consider this carefully before following this route and always endeavour to seek independent financial advice before making a final decision.

A similar option is a <u>Debt Management Plan</u>. This is a service that has to be offered by a licensed Debt Management company, the licence being given by the Office of Fair Trading. Although most companies will charge you for this, there are charities that will do this for free including StepChange, Debt Charity and Payplan.

Administration Orders

If you have a county court judgement against you for a debt of less than £5000, you can apply for an administration order against you to the court. The court decides what a fair monthly amount is depending on your income, and can reduce the total amount to be paid. Once in place, as long as you make payments, the creditor cannot take any further action against you.

Individual Voluntary Arrangements (IVA)

This is a court-backed arrangement to pay off an agreed amount of your debt (i.e. a reduced amount) over a defined period. This is obviously an attractive option if you have debts (and many of the 'for profit' debt advice companies sell their services on this) but there are drawbacks. Firstly, it is only really an option if you do have funds available each month to pay at the agreed amount. Secondly, IVA's have to be set up by a qualified insolvency practitioner whose fees tend to be high. Finally, your creditors can block IVA agreements – they are, after all losing out by the arrangement.

There are also Fast Track Voluntary Arrangements (FTVA) if you have already been made bankrupt. These are available through application to the Official Receiver.

Debt Relief Orders (DRO)

These are an alternative to the 'full' bankruptcy route if things get really bad. They are designed for people who owe less than £15,000 and cannot afford to pay more than £50 per month to creditors. You should also have assets worth less than £300 and have a car worth less than £1000. The fees are lower than bankruptcy. If you get one you are protected from your creditors by the courts and you are discharged from your debts after 12 months. You get a DRO through the Official Receiver, but an application has to be made by an authorised debt advisor. The cost is £90 but it comes with restrictions; you cannot borrow more than £500 without telling the lender about your DRO, act as the director of a company and create, manage or promote a company without the court's permission, normally for a period of 12 months. The DRO stays on your credit record for 6 years.

Bankruptcy

If you have large debts and no money to pay them (or so little it will take many years to pay them off) then bankruptcy may be an option. This can take away the pressures of creditors. You are allowed to keep certain things, like household goods and money to live on, whilst the rest of your debts are written off. When the bankruptcy is over you are able to make a fresh start. Creditors have to stop most actions though bailiffs may still be able to seize goods. Bankruptcy is expensive, however, and there are on-going effects on your credit record similar to those discussed with DROs.

Note that creditors can apply to make you bankrupt as a way of securing at least some of the debt owed to them, though this is generally only as a last resort.

Harassment

Even if you are in debt you should not be subject to harassment or threats (the latter particularly being true of loan sharks). If you feel you are then contact the CAB or even the police.

Credit History

There is no such thing as a credit blacklist but it is true that if you do not pay your debts you may find it difficult to get credit in the future. If you apply for credit, the lender will search the records of county and high court judgements, bankruptcy orders, IVAs, DROs and the like with the credit ratings agency. These records usually last for 6 years.

Whilst everyone has the right to refuse you credit you do have a right to ask why. You can also check your record with the credit reference agencies for a fee of £2 and a right to challenge an incorrect record.

Conclusions

Being in debt can be frightening and stressful. As you will have seen from this section, however, there are a number of actions you can take. The key thing is always to talk to your creditors. There are also places you can go for free advice, particularly from bodies like the CAB and the National Debt Line. They are non-judgemental and will be sympathetic. They are there to help you, so come out of hiding and deal with your debt head on and be free from worry and anxiety.

Chapter 8

The Benefits of Financial Freedom

Imagine a situation where you are totally in charge of your finances.

You are no longer worried about paying bills, concerned about the amount of debt that you have accumulated, wondering what will happen with your job, whether you might be made redundant. You no longer look at your children and worry that you are not going to be able to help them in the future – with their education, careers, with getting them onto the property ladder. You can help them, help the rest of your family, give generously to charity, and purchase anything you want. Your future is secure, you have no doubt that you will have plenty of money to live on in your retirement – in fact you are looking forward to it because of all the leisure activities you are going to enjoy and all the travelling you are going to do.

Is that a nice picture?

We are sure that it is. That is what financial freedom means.

It is worth striving for, isn't it?

But is this realistic? Is it just a pipe-dream?

We believe this book will have given you the tools you need to obtain financial freedom. It should have enabled you to alter the way you see things, helped you change your thought patterns; helped you have the right attitudes and given you ideas and information about creating and retaining wealth.

So what is stopping you from achieving your dreams of financial wealth and freedom?

Well, many people have excuses as to why they cannot fulfil their dreams, some of these include:

- Wealthy, financially secure people are cleverer, have more skills, have had a better start in life and are luckier than me;
- It's easy to get wealthy if you have money to start with. Everyone is better off than me
- Being wealthy is wrong anyway

Are these excuses really valid?

Let us look at each one in turn.

Wealthy, financially secure people are cleverer, have more skills, have had a better start in life and are luckier than me

Think of the wealthy people that you know personally and ask yourself whether this is really true. With the exception of the rare, gifted entrepreneur or sportsman, wealthy people are nothing special; they are, in fact, invariably very ordinary people. You might look at them and ask; 'how did they get so rich?' And, almost invariably, the answer is simple; common sense and the right attitude to money and wealth is what got them there.

It's easy to get wealthy if you have money to start with. Everyone is better off than me

Again, this is sometimes true – but probably less often than you think. In fact you do not need to have huge amounts of money to have financial freedom; you just need to use what you have very wisely. Charles Dickens, writing in a period where ordinary people started to get wealthy for the first time – the Victorian era – was an astute observer of the condition of his characters. His observations are as relevant in the 21st century as they were in then (19th century). An oft quoted example is Mr Micawber's recipe for happiness in *David Copperfield*:

> *"Annual income twenty pounds, annual expenditure nineteen pounds, nineteen shillings and six [pence], result happiness. Annual income twenty pounds, annual expenditure twenty pounds ought and six, result misery."*

This still certainly rings true in today's world. Live within your means, budget carefully, and whilst you may not yet be wealthy, you will already have achieved a degree of financial freedom. Similarly in *Great Expectations*, Pip's on moving to London lived an extravagant lifestyle which has parallels in today's world of "buy now; pay later" mentality.

> *"So now, as an infallible way of making little ease great ease, I began to contract a quantity of debt."*

There is such a temptation today to make '*little ease great ease*' by the liberal use of credit cards, store cards, loans etc. to buy up the fruits of the consumer society but you are essentially spending tomorrow's money today – and what happens if tomorrow's money does not come in or you overreach yourself. You are in Micawber's misery.

We are not saying that you should be a Scrooge, to use another Dickens' character, but that you should be careful with your money, treat it like water in a desert, conserve it and use it wisely. Debt is not necessarily a bad thing if it is obtained for a purpose i.e. to buy your house, to invest in property or a business – that is debt that will give you future returns.

So being financial free is not necessarily about how much money you have but how wisely you use what you have got.

Being wealthy is wrong anyway

Isn't money the root of all evil?

Well, no, and not just because this is one of the most misquoted parts of the Bible. What 1 Timothy 6:10 actually says is:

> For the love of money is a root of all kinds of evils. It is through this craving that some have wandered away from the faith and pierced themselves with many pangs

English Standard Version (©2001)

There is nothing wrong with money and wealth; it is the love of it and the ruthless pursuit of it which destroys people. To gather wealth honestly and then use it wisely for the good of your family, society and yourself cannot surely be criticised?

So we ask again, what is stopping you from achieving your dreams of financial wealth and freedom?

Nothing we hope!

Good luck on your journey.

Chapter 9

The Way Forward

Goal Setting

"If a man knows not what harbor he seeks,
any wind is the right wind."—Seneca

Goal setting is a crucial component of your Action Plan. Effectively identifying and aligning both your personal and professional life goals is essential. If you don't know EXACTLY where it is you want to go in life, you won't be able to write yourself a road map to get there.

Establishing BIG GOALS are important; if they are too small you wouldn't stretch yourself and your capabilities.

S.M.A.R.T—is an easy way to remember the components you need to consider when setting your goals: Specific, Measurable, Attainable, Realistic, Timely.

SPECIFIC: Make sure you are extremely specific when mapping out your goals. Specific goals have a much greater chance of being accomplished than general goals. To set a specific goal you must answer the six "W" questions:

- WHO: Who are the people involved?
- WHAT: What am I trying to achieve?
- WHEN: Set a time frame.

- WHERE: Identify the location/s.
- WHY: What are the benefits of accomplishing the goal?
- WHICH: Identify the requirements and any limitations.

Example: 1

A **general** goal is; "I want to invest some money in Real Estate."

A **specific** goal would be; "Build a property portfolio by researching residential real estate market; allocate £30,000 of investment capital to the first property. Make my first purchase within 8 months; then purchase second property once there is capital growth in the first to fund the second property's deposit."

Example: 2

A **general** goal is; "I want to invest some money in the Share Market."

A **specific** goal would be; "Research the share market, allocate £10,000 of investment capital to blue chip shares and begin trading within 3 months."

Example: 3

A **general** goal is; "I want to create a passive income on the Internet via network marketing."

A **specific** goal would be; "Research network marketing, join a networking group, create a down line of 10 people within 3 months."

- MEASURABLE: Measuring your progress as you move towards each goal enables you to keep inspired and focused. To determine if your goal is measurable, ask yourself questions such as . . . . How much? How many? How will I know when it is complete?

- ATTAINABLE: Many people fail to strive towards what they really want as they let limiting beliefs stifle their growth, they believe they can't achieve the success they desire because they don't have the skills required. Goals often seem too hard at the initial stage but once you begin to figure out how to achieve them, you develop the attitude, abilities, skills and financial know how to attain them.

You will start seeing previously overlooked opportunities to bring your closer to your desired goal. You can achieve any goal you set when planned wisely and established with a reasonable time frame. Goals that seem impossible to achieve would suddenly become attainable, not because your goals shrunk but because you grew and expanded to match them.

When you build your self-image and accept that you are worthy and able to attain your goals nothing will be able to stop your progress and fulfillment of your goals of financial freedom.

- REALISTIC: To be realistic, a goal must have objectives that can reasonably be attained. It must be realistic in all aspects of the word. If someone sets a goal of losing 15kgs in one week, that would be an unrealistic goal under any circumstances, however, what may be realistic to one person may be unrealistic to another. Realistic does not mean it must be something you can do already; setting goals a little out of your reach will ensure you continually grow and build new skills.
- TIMELY: When goals have realistic time frames it is certain that the goal will be achieved. If the goal has no specific time frame things will get in the way of your success and your goal would not get achieved. A fixed deadline compels and motivates you into action. It the goal is not met by the deadline do not be disheartened, simply set a new date.

Action Plan

Goals	Objectives	Date
Lifestyle Goals	Design list of ultimate Lifestyle goals.	_/_/_.
Professional Goals	Design list of ultimate Career goals.	_/_/_.
Investment Portfolio	Identify investment vehicles that are aligned with your Lifestyle & Professional goals; and list them out.	_/_/_.
Research Phase	Source out educational and/or professional services that will support you in attaining your Lifestyle, Professional and investment goals.	_/_/_.
Personal Budget	Create a budget with your new lifestyle goals in mind.	_/_/_.
Business Budget	Create a budget with your new professional goals in mind.	_/_/_.
Take Action	Date/s on which each goal listed above has to be initiated and achieved.	_/_/_.
Review Dates	Set regular (quarterly) review dates to revise your Action Plan.	_/_/_.

Book & Website Reference Guide

BOOKS

- "The Coming Wealth Transfer"by Matthew Ashimolowo.
- "The Richest Man in Babylon" by George S.Clason.
- "Rich Dad, Poor Dad" by Robert Kiyosaki.
- "Think and Grow Rich" by Napoleon Hill.
- "Trade your way to Financial Freedom" by Van K Tharp.
- "The Disciplined Trader" by Mark Douglas.
- "The Winning Investment Habits of Warren Buffett and George Soros" by Mark Tier.
- "Science of Getting Rich" by Wallace D Wattles.
- "Real Estate Mistakes" by Neil Jenman.
- "Positive Cash Flow in Property" by Margaret Lomas.
- Tax, The FT guide 2011-12 by Sara Williams and John Bloxham

SOME USEFUL WEBSITES

http://www.clickpaid.com/?r=123492
http://www.profitwealthclub.com/?ref=Destiny
http://www.forex.com/uk/land-trade-gen.html?src=201304C NS1702&gclid=CP2h4eSdgrcCFSbHtAod-xkAAA
www.londonstockexchange.com
http://www.google.com/finance
http://investors.assetz.co.uk/
www.dogsofthedow.com
www.investopedia.com
www.bloomberg.com

www.adviceguide.org.uk
www.hmrc.gov.uk
www.thebfa.org/
http://ukfo.org/
www.franchiseinfo.co.uk
www.thefranchisemagazine.net
www.theukfranchisedirectory.net
http://www.franchise.org/
www.gov.uk/options-for-paying-off-your-debts/overview
www.nationaldebtline.co.uk
www.globaltaxnetwork.co.uk
www.taxresearch.org.uk
www.voa.gov.uk

Beginners guide to working for yourself /starting up a business—
www.hmrc.gov.uk/startingup/index.htm

FREEBIES

EBooks: Wealth Creation—http://www.mymillionairebuddy.com/

Conclusion

Imagine a table in front of you filled with an elaborately prepared meal of your choice (your favourite food or the type you have always dreamt of eating).

Did your mouth water when we mentioned this to you? Do you realise that your mouth watered simply because of this suggestion or thought we put into your mind. This physiological reaction in your body was instantaneous.

Why are we telling you this?

Well, we found that the main difference between the wealthy and poor is in their thought patterns and choices they make. For you to attain the financial freedom that you desire you must condition your mind not to settle for mediocrity. Until you make up your mind to be financially free, nothing will change for you. If you wonder whether you need to recondition your mindset to that of a wealthy person, the answer is yes.

You can start slowly with the wealth strategies that you are familiar with and then progress to more intermediate and advanced strategies as you build up your confidence. Failure is not merely attempting and not succeeding . . . but also not starting out at all. You have so much information at your fingertips that you have no excuse for not making a start on your goals.

By challenging yourself and your thought patterns you will find yourself moving forward. You must choose investment vehicles that best fit your lifestyle and stick with them, once you do this, there is no stopping you.

God has invested so much in you, it is your sole responsibility to utilise the untapped resources inside of you. You must not depart this world without leaving a lasting impact on your generation and those after them. You must positively influence your successors to become achievers in their own right.

Make your life a journey of purpose . . .

Thanks so much for reading this book. We hope you enjoyed it and have learned all you need to know in order to effectively create and retain wealth.

We would like to wish you the best of luck and every success in your quest to attain financial freedom and Financial Success.

If you have found this book useful, kindly provide your reviews on the website you purchased a copy of this book from or the various publishing platforms such as Amazon, CreateSpace and Lulu.

Other Books by Authors

A simple Guide to UK Immigration

The Beginners' Guide to Writing, Self-Publishing and Marketing a Book

Become All That God Has Created You To Be

You Are Blessed

Hearing God's Voice

Purpose2Destiny TK Limited

P O BOX 3162

Romford

RM3 9WR

United Kingdom

www.ingramcontent.com/pod-product-compliance
Lightning Source LLC
Chambersburg PA
CBHW060033210326
41520CB00009B/1106